Getting IT Right

information and communications technology

Skills Book I | Levels 3-4

Alison Page and Tristram Shepard

First published in 1999 by:
Stanley Thornes (Publishers) Ltd
Ellenborough House
Wellington Street
CHELTENHAM
GL50 1YW

A catalogue record for this book is available from the British Library.

ISBN 0 7487 4421 5

99 00 01 02 03 / 10 9 8 7 6 5 4 3 2 1

Designed and typeset by Krystyna Hewitt
Artwork by OXFORD designers & illustrators and John Fowler
Printed and bound in Spain by Cayfosa, Barcelona

Acknowledgements

The authors would like to acknowledge, with thanks, the assistance of Carol Webb in checking the content of this book.

The following are trademarks of Microsoft Corporation: *Windows 3.0*, *Windows 3.1*, *Windows 95*, *Windows 98*, *Windows NT*, *PowerPoint*, *Encarta*. Screen shots of all Microsoft products are reprinted with permission from Microsoft Corporation.

Apple and Macintosh are trademarks of Apple Computer, Inc.

Corel and *WordPerfect*, *CorelDRAW* and *Corel GALLERY Magic* are trademarks or registered trademarks of Corel Corporation or Corel Corporation Limited. Screen shots are © 1999 Corel Corporation and Corel Corporation Limited, reprinted by permission.

Netscape *Navigator* is part of Netscape *Communicator* which are trademarks of Netscape Communications Corporation.

Mach Turtles *Logo* is a trademark of Mach Turtles Software Inc.

Adobe and *Photoshop* are trademarks of Adobe Systems Inc.

Total Virus Defense is a trademark of Network Associates Inc.

AltaVista is a trademark of Compaq Corporation. Screen shots are reprinted with permission from Compaq Corporation.

Yahoo is a registered trademark of Yahoo Inc.

Excite and *WebCrawler* are trademarks of Excite Inc.

Lycos is a registered trademark of Carnegie Mellon University.

The publishers are grateful to the following for permission to reproduce photographs or other illustrative material:
Apple: p. 8 (left), p. 9 (centre)
Canterbury Christchurch College: p. 47
Cephas Picture Library: p. 11 (bottom)
Ecoscene (Mike Whittle): p. 51 (top)
Eidos Interactive UK: p. 83
Evening Standard (D Jones): p. 60
IBM: pp. 4, 5 (bottom), 10, 144
Janine Weidel Photolibrary: p. 113
John Birdsall Photography: p. 18 (left)
Leslie Garland Picture Library: pp. 40 (E Ryle-Hodges), 100 (bottom left and bottom centre)
Martyn Chillmaid: pp. 5 (top left), 21, 32 (left), 34, 51 (bottom), 80, 81 (centre), 93, 128, 135
Mercedes: p. 32
Microsoft: p. 9 (top)
PC World Business Direct: pp. 5 (centre top and centre left), 8 (right), 12, 15, 67
Pictor Uniphoto: p. 137
Rex Features: pp. 5 (centre right – ITN), 61 (DPP)
Scholastic Children's Books (Martin Brown): p. 100 (top)
Science Photolibrary (Andrew Syred): p. 99
Science Pictures Ltd: p. 43
Sky: p. 32
Stockmarket: p. 18 (right)
TRIP/H Rogers: pp. 8 (centre), 9 (bottom), 19 (top), 50
Virgin: p. 32

All other photographs from STP Archive.

Contents

Introduction 4

Starting Up

Introduction 8
1. What's in store? 10
2. Software 12
3. Safety matters 14
4. Keeping it secure 16
5. IT for everyone 18

Unit 1 The User Interface

Introduction 20
1. On the desktop 22
2. Starting up 24
3. Opening the windows 26
4. In single file 28
5. Which Windows? 30

Unit 2 Graphics

Introduction 32
1. Opening up 34
2. Save it or lose it 36
3. Putting on the style 38
4. An open and shut case 40
5. Any colour you like 42
6. Words and pictures 44
7. Self-selection 46
8. On the move 48

Unit 3 Word Processing

Introduction 50
1. On keyboards 52
2. Save it. Print it. Close it. 54
3. Putting on the style (1) 56
4. Putting on the style (2) 58
5. Spelling test 60
6. The text files 62

Unit 4 Presentation

Introduction 64
1. Using clip art 66
2. Swap shop 68
3. All together now 70
4. Many media 72
5. Getting it together (1) 74
6. Getting it together (2) 76
7. Power presentation 78

Unit 5 In Control

Introduction 80
1. At the interface 82
2. Turning turtle 84
3. In command 86
4. Now in colour 88
5. Getting into shape 90

Unit 6 Searching for Information

Introduction 92
1. Finding your way around 94
2. Desperately seeking… 96
3. I've found it! 98
4. On the record 100

Unit 7 On the Internet

Introduction 102
1. Just browsing 104
2. Link up 106
3. Really useful engines 108
4. Dinomaniac search (1) 110
5. Dinomaniac search (2) 112
6. Working with web sites 114

Unit 8 Electronic Mail

Introduction 116
1. Where it's @ 118
2. Packaging and posting 120
3. Dear... 122
4. Open the box 124
5. Becoming attached 126

Unit 9 Spreadsheets

Introduction 128
1. Spreading the work 130
2. What are your values? 132
3. Getting your sums right 134
4. Making it look good 136
5. Over and over again 138
6. Say it with graphs 140
7. It's magic! 142

Index 144

Getting IT Right

Welcome to Getting IT Right. This book will help you to develop your skills in using information and communication technologies.

Learning about IT

Information and communication technologies include things like computers and other electronic devices such as cameras, scanners, videos, faxes and photocopiers.

These days such devices are becoming very familiar in homes and at work. They can help us to live and work more effectively and enjoyably.

You need to learn how, when and when not to use these new electronic devices. It's important that you get used to a wide range of computer programs. These will help you to do many things more quickly and easily.

Remember that you can apply what you learn in this book to all your school subjects. Don't wait for your teachers to tell you to use the technology. Can you see a way in which using a computer or some other electronic device would help you to get the job done better? Don't hesitate to ask if you can do it that way!

CD-ROM drive – for reading or loading files

Floppy disk drive – used for loading or storing information on a 3.5 inch disk

Monitor or **VDU** (Visual Display Unit) – used to display the electronic information produced by the computer

CPU (Central Processing Unit) – this is where information is electronically processed

Keyboard – used to type in commands

Mouse – for moving an arrow or pointer around the screen

Digital camera – used to get electronic images directly into a computer

Fax machine

Satellites – used to transmit digital information across the world

Scanner – used to get existing photographs and text into a computer

This book is mainly about using computers. Books 2 and 3 in the series look at a wider range of communication devices

Printer – used to print out images and text onto paper or film

Modem – used to transfer data down telephone lines

Portable *lap-top* **computer** – for use anywhere

About the units

This book is divided into nine units. There is also an introductory section called *Starting Up*. If you're new to computers it would be a good idea to begin by working through *Starting Up* and the first three units. After that you should be able to do the remaining units in any order.

Each unit is based on a different software package. You may not have exactly the same package used in the illustrations but you are sure to have something very similar. Your teacher will tell you about any important differences.

Each unit starts with its own introduction. This helps to explain the sort of everyday problems and situations in which you are likely to find it helpful to use IT. The introduction also makes it clear what the targets for the unit are, that is what you should know about and be able to do by the time you have worked through the unit. You will also find some suggestions for how you might use the software in your other subjects.

Working through the pages

You will need to work through the numbered pages in each unit in order. In some lessons you might get through several pages quite quickly, especially if you've used a similar package before. It may be that you used computers a lot in your previous school. Perhaps you've got one at home. Though maybe it's been quite a while since you last used a particular piece of software. You might find some of the early pages very useful for some revision.

Each double-page is self-contained. Read it through first, or listen carefully as your teacher takes you through it. The next step is to experiment with the various actions needed to make the program work, such as:

● finding menus
● clicking in the right place
● dragging things across the screen.

It takes a while to get used to some of these!

In particular, look out for instructions on the page which follow coloured buttons. For example:

● Click on **New** in the **File** menu

Make sure you try these things out. Don't be afraid to make mistakes – it won't damage the computer!

In **Unit 1** you'll learn about the **user interface**

Unit **2** explores **graphics** packages

Unit **3** is about **word processing**

Controlling things by writing exact instructions is the subject of **Unit 5**

Unit 4 shows how to combine text, pictures and sounds together in a **presentation**

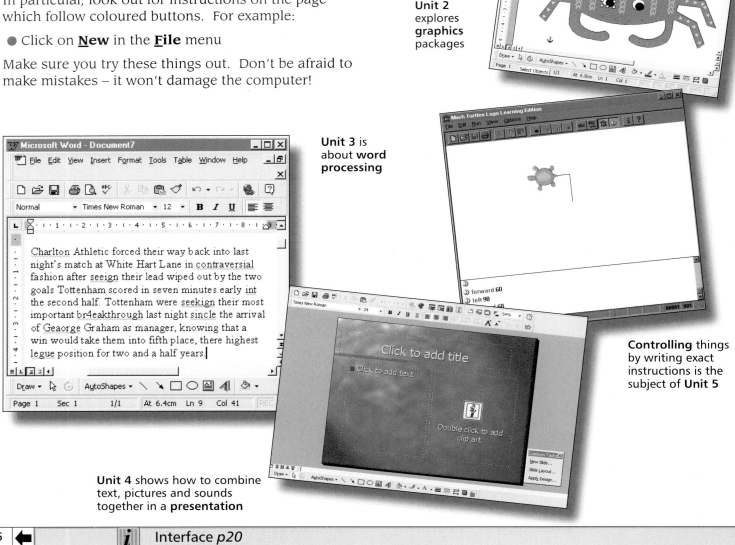

Charlton Athletic forced their way back into last night's match at White Hart Lane in contraversial fashion after seeign their lead wiped out by the two goals Tottenham scored in seven minutes early int the second half. Tottenham were seekign their most important br4eakthrough last night sincle the arrival of Geaorge Graham as manager, knowing that a win would take them into fifth place, there highest legue position for two and a half years.

WHAT YOU HAVE TO DO

On every right-hand page you'll find a very important section in the bottom corner called *What you have to do.* These are activities you should do after you have experimented for a while and have got to know what you are doing. Your teacher will tell you which ones to do – some might be done after the lesson and others are for those who are speeding ahead.

Always remember to save the work you do on the computer. You should also print your work out as often as possible. Keep it in a special IT folder.

You'll also find sections on the left and right of some pages that have a grey colour background. These contain extra information that you might find interesting – things like keyboard short-cuts and more about how computers work.

Unit 6 is all about **finding information**

Unit 7 will explain what you can do on the **Internet**

In **Unit 8** you'll get to send, and maybe receive, some **e-mails**

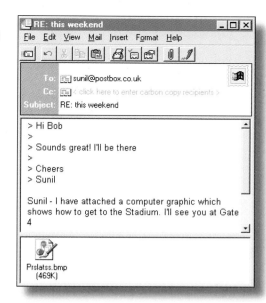

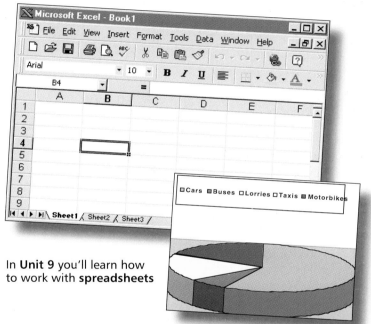

In **Unit 9** you'll learn how to work with **spreadsheets**

Applying what you've learned

At the end of each unit your teacher will probably give you a special project to undertake. You'll be given a problem to solve and will be expected to use the computer to help you. To begin with you'll need to plan out what you need to do and when. At the end you'll need to evaluate your work.

This project will help you and your teacher to work out how well you are doing. It will show up your strengths and weaknesses and provide you with some useful targets for improvement in the next unit you do.

Good luck with your work – we hope you manage to ***Get IT Right!***

Starting Up

This section provides important information about how to use computers. You will need to remember these things in all your IT lessons and whenever you are using a computer in other subject lessons.

On Target

This introductory unit will tell you what you need to know to be able to understand and apply the different units that follow.

You will learn:

- how to work safely and sensibly with the computer
- the meaning of basic computer terms such as hardware and software
- how computer equipment is used
- about making sure that everyone gets proper access to computers.

On each page there is some suggested work for you to do. Complete the tasks that your teacher tells you to do. Remember to keep the work you produce in a special IT folder.

As you work through the different units, you will probably find that you need to look back at this section for reference.

Hardware

Computers are everywhere. You see them at home, at school, in shops and in offices.

New types of computer are always being developed. You will see them advertised in newspapers and magazines.

Some computers are designed to do just one task – for example to play games. Other computers can be used for a wide range of different tasks.

All the computers shown below are different from each other. But all computers are built along the same lines. Understanding how computer systems are put together will help you to learn how to use them.

The different items which fit together to make the computer system are called **hardware**.

Storage *p10*   The Internet *p102*

Controlling the Computer ■

Information needs to be put into the computer to tell it what to do. You can use a **keyboard** and **mouse** to do this.

When you use a computer to play a game you might use a **joystick** instead. It tells the computer the actions you want to take in the game.

Processing the Information ■

The computer **processor** is where the computer does all its work. You can't see the processor because it is inside the computer's casing. New computers usually have more powerful processors. They can do more things and work more quickly.

Seeing what Happens ■

You need to see the results of the computer's work.

You look at the **monitor** screen all the time you are using the computer to see what is going on.

A **printer** gives you results on paper.

Saving your Work ■

You need to save information and instructions for use at another time. If you don't save your work it will be lost. One way of storing your work is to save it on a floppy disk.

Computer Networks ■

Computers can be set up to send electronic messages to other computers.

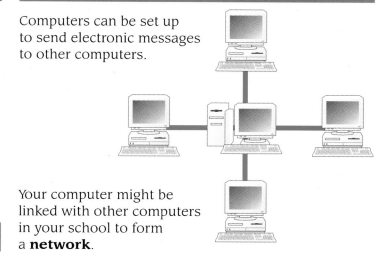

Your computer might be linked with other computers in your school to form a **network**.

It might be linked to other computers all over the world by the **Internet**.

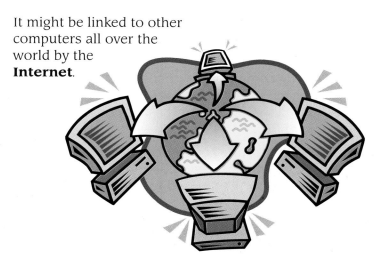

WHAT YOU HAVE TO DO

1. Study a computer system you use at school. Find out the following:

   ■ does it have a keyboard and mouse?

   ■ what printer is it connected to?

   ■ is it linked to other computers in the school to make a network?

   ■ does it have a connection to the Internet?

2. Draw a diagram of this computer system. Write on your picture the names of the different parts described on this page.

Keep your answers and your drawing neatly in your IT folder.

1. What's in store?

On this page you will learn about the different ways that you can store your work. Storing your work safely is important – otherwise you will lose what you have done.

Your teacher will tell you which ways to save your work on the computer at school.

Storage

While you are using the computer, all its work is electrical. The words you type in at the keyboard are stored in the computer as electrical signals. The pictures on the screen, and the sounds the computer makes, are the result of electrical signals.

When the computer is turned off the electricity disappears. If you don't save your work it will also disappear when the computer is switched off.

Computer **storage** is how you save and keep your work when the computer is either switched off or being used for something else.

Floppy disks

A **floppy disk** doesn't seem very floppy. That's because it is held in a hard protective case. Inside the case is a floppy circle of plastic.

Floppy disks are cheap, light and convenient. You can copy your work onto a floppy disk at the end of a lesson and put it in your bag. Next lesson you might be sitting at a different computer. Just put your disk in the new computer and you will be able to get on with your work again.

To use a floppy disk, put it in the disk drive of the computer.

Make sure you take care of your floppy disk. Don't lose it!

Stacy
7B

Hard disks

The **hard disk** is a pile of metal disks held inside the computer. You can't see it unless you take the computer to bits.

The hard disk will store much more than a floppy disk. If you have a computer at home you might use the hard disk to store the things you do on that computer. However, it isn't a good idea to use the hard disk at school to store your school work.

Why not? The main reason is because you might work at a different computer another day. Also, everyone who uses that computer can get at the work you saved. They might delete your work, accidentally or on purpose.

If you are going to use a floppy disk, put a label on the disk with your name and class written on it. If you have more than one disk, give each one a different label

CD-ROMs

A **CD-ROM** will store a lot more than a floppy disk. You can store a whole set of encyclopaedias on a single CD-ROM. But you can't use a standard CD-ROM to store your work. You can't put new information onto a CD-ROM. The pictures and words stored on the CD-ROM were fixed on at the factory.

To use a CD-ROM, put it in the CD drive of the computer.

Network storage

If you work at a computer that is connected to a **network** then you can save your work *over the network*.

At the centre of the network is a computer called the **File Server**. You can send your work in electronic form down the wire to the file server to save it and store it there. You can then get to your work from any computer on the network.

To connect up to the network you have to give a **password**. Because nobody else knows your password, nobody else can get at your work.

New types of storage

An interesting thing about computers is that new things are being invented all the time. Storage is no exception. Your computer at school or at home might have a type of storage not shown here.

For example there are several types of high-capacity disk. These are used through special drives that you can buy. One of these disks can hold as much as a hard disk and people use them to back up everything on the computer. They can also be used for general storage. These are often called *Zip Drives*, though there are also other makes.

New versions of the CD-ROM are also being developed. These devices allow you to save new information onto the CD yourself.

If you are interested in new developments, read computer magazines or news items in the papers.

WHAT YOU HAVE TO DO

1. Write notes about how you are going to store your work. Name the device you are going to use. Say what precautions you are going to take to keep your work safe.

2. Ask your school librarian, or ask at the public library, to show you what computer CD-ROMs are available.

   ■ Can you spot any which might help you with your schoolwork?

   ■ Write down the names of 3 you could borrow.

   ■ How long can you borrow them for?

   ■ Do you have to pay or leave a deposit?

   Write notes on what you find out.

3. Name three different ways of storing computer information. Read through a computer magazine and cut out adverts for storage devices. Make notes to go with the pictures about how much each device can hold.

Make sure you put all your work into your IT folder.

2. Software

It's the software that tells the computer what to do. Different software programmes enable you to do different things.

Your teacher will tell you the names of the different software packages you will be using in school.

Software

The instructions that make a computer work are called **software**. A simple computer like a calculator or a games console can only use one type of software and only do one thing. But a personal computer like the one you use at school can use many different software packages.

When you want to do some work on the computer you have to decide what software to use. You start up the software package and the computer is ready to do the work.

On page 24 you will learn how to start up software packages. As you work through this book you will learn to use many different software packages to do all sorts of work.

The same computer can do many different tasks. It depends what software it is using

Where software is stored

Most software is written by professional programmers. You buy a copy of the software on a floppy disk or a CD-ROM. Then you *install it* onto the hard disk of your computer. You can then start it up whenever you like.

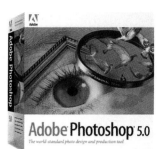

Your computer at school probably has several different software packages already available on its hard disk.

If your computer is connected to a network you might be able to use software from the file server at the centre of the network.

It is also possible to download software from the Internet.

Types of software

In this book you will learn about the main types of software, such as:

● **Graphics** software. This lets you draw pictures.
● **Word processing** software. This lets you prepare text.
● **Spreadsheet** software. This lets you make calculations.
● **Web browser** software. This lets you use the Internet.

 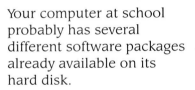

The Windows interface

Nowadays most software packages use the Microsoft *Windows* interface, or something very similar.

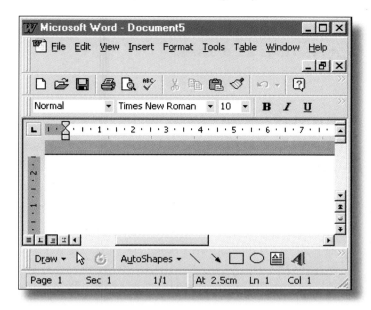

Windows packages use pictures and menus to help you give instructions to the computer.

All Windows packages are designed to look very similar. This makes it easier to learn how to use them. You soon get used to the way they work.

There is more on the Windows interface on page 30.

Compatibility

Different types of computer work in different ways. Software that works in one computer won't necessarily work in another. You can't always take a disk out of one computer (say at school) and put it in another computer (say at home).

If two computers can use the same software then they are said to be **compatible**.

On the whole, all of the main software packages are just as good as each other and work in very similar ways. Whatever packages you use at school, you should be able to follow the examples given in this book.

Loading software

When you *load* (or **open**) a software package it is copied from storage into the electronic working memory of your computer. Once the software has been loaded, the computer can use it to do work for you.

The electronic memory of the computer is sometimes called RAM. Computers with more RAM can load larger software packages.

Modern computers can load several different software packages at the same time – you will learn more about this on page 68.

When you have finished working with the package you *close it down* (often called **Quit** or **Exit**). When a package is closed it is in storage. You cannot use a package which is closed to do any work. When you close a package the work you have done with that package is also closed down. If the work has not been saved it will be lost.

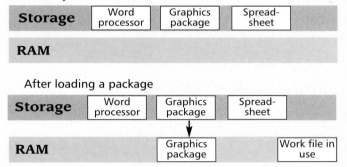

WHAT YOU HAVE TO DO

1. **Write down the names of the packages you will be using.**

   ■ **What graphics package?**

   ■ **What word processor package?**

   ■ **What spreadsheet package?**

   ■ **What Internet package?**

2. **If you have a computer at home, find out if it is compatible with the computer you use at school. Does it use any of the same software packages? If not, which ones does it use? Write them down.**

Keep your work in your IT folder.

3. Safety matters

You might not think that working with computers could be dangerous! On this page you will learn the rules of good working practice.

Remember you need to follow these rules at all times – not just in your IT lessons.

Safety

Don't worry – a computer isn't a dangerous machine. Even so, there are some simple rules you should follow to make sure that accidents don't happen.

The common sense rules of safety are called **good working practice**. If you work with a computer you must observe the rules of good working practice. In school, and later in college and in work, you won't get very far unless you know how to work safely.

Risks to avoid

You have to make sure that you don't:

- hurt yourself or anyone else
- damage the computer equipment
- lose or spoil information and software.

Safe working practices help avoid all three risks.

Your health

People who use a computer a lot sometimes complain about:
- back-ache
- eye strain
- aching hands.

Other people sometimes worry that there might be radiation coming out of computer and TV screens. None of these problems will affect you from making use of a computer at school. But if you have particular medical concerns, for example a bad back or epilepsy, then please tell your teacher right away.

Keeping yourself safe

The computer is an electrical machine. Like anything else which is connected to the mains you should treat it with respect. That means:

- don't open up a computer case, particularly when it is switched on
- don't put anything into the computer or any of its sockets
- ask a teacher before you plug or un-plug a computer and make sure you don't have wet hands.

The computer might be a fairly heavy machine. Don't try to move it about. If you are asked to move a computer, pick it up carefully, bending your knees not your back.

Computer rooms are often very crowded. Be considerate to others in the limited space.

- Tuck your bag out of the way.
- Don't run or throw things.
- Keep your chair in one place.

i Security *p16*

Keeping the computer safe ■

If computer equipment is broken at your school, then you will be the one to suffer. You might have to share equipment instead of having a computer to yourself. You might lose work if the computer is broken.

Knocking, moving or shaking equipment is obviously a bad idea. So are *do-it-yourself* repairs and alterations.

If something goes wrong – for example you put a disk in the wrong way round and can't get it out again – then ask a teacher or technician for help. Don't try to fix it yourself first!

Food and drink should be kept well away from computers. A cup of coffee spilled into a computer can cause literally thousands of pounds worth of damage.

Looking after floppy disks ■

Floppy disks are a good way to save your work. But they need to be looked after carefully. There are many ways in which a floppy disk can be spoiled and all your work lost.

- Wet and sticky substances, like drinks and sweets, will spoil a floppy disk if they get onto it.
- If the disk gets too hot it will literally melt – don't leave it near a radiator.
- If the disk gets bent or cracked it will be useless – don't put it at the bottom of your bag and then tread on it.
- Strong magnetic fields will wipe everything off your disk – and beware, TVs and monitor screens can generate invisible magnetic fields. So can security systems at libraries and airports.

Look after your floppy disks. They are safest when stored in a protective disk case.

Computer viruses

A computer **virus** is a hidden computer program. Practical jokers write these programs and hide them on disks or on the Internet. You can accidentally copy the virus onto your computer along with software or information.

Some viruses just print silly messages on your computer screen – irritating but fairly harmless. Others can cause your computer to break down or all your work to be deleted. A virus can cause you a lot of problems. Remember:

- be careful what you copy onto your computer
- never copy your own software onto the computers at school
- only buy software from reputable companies and shops.

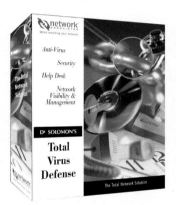

You can buy software that scans your computer and disks for viruses. Your school probably has this software set up already. But beware, new viruses are being written all the time. The scan could miss one.

WHAT YOU HAVE TO DO

1. **If you are using floppy disks to store your work, make notes about where you are going to keep the disk and how you are going to avoid it getting damaged.**

2. **Your school probably has a set of rules about how to work in the IT room. With a partner, discuss ways to improve them. If there aren't any rules then try to write some.**

Make sure you keep a copy of all your work in your IT folder.

4. Keeping it secure

**This page is about keeping your IT work safe, and private.
Above all, remember to save your work regularly.**

Security

The electronic information, or **data**, held on a computer is often very important. A computer could store:

- a list of doctor's appointments
- the amount of money held in a bank account
- a secret industrial formula
- the script of the next episode of *EastEnders*.

For all types of people who use computers it is important that data is secure.

Your computer, or your computer disk, holds information which is very important to you – your own work. A piece of work on your computer could represent hours of work. The last thing you want is for it to be spoiled or lost.

Computer security is about ensuring that the information on your computer is kept **safe** and **private**.

Safety

If data is **safe** it will not be lost or spoiled. This means that the time you have spent working on a task will not be wasted. Data can be lost through:

- computer faults
- human errors
- deliberate actions.

Privacy

If data is **private** then it cannot be seen by anyone who is not supposed to see it. You might want to make sure that your school work can't be copied and handed in by someone else. In the world of work, computers often hold important secrets. These need to be kept private.

Files

When you save a piece of work, for example onto a disk, you save it as a **file**. Every computer file has its own **file name**. This tells it apart from all the other pieces of work.

Saving *p36*

Mistakes you might make

Here are some of the mistakes that are easy to make – and that might lose you a whole lesson of work.

Forget to save

If you forget to save your work before you shut down the computer, it will be lost.

Delete too much

Computers let you make changes and corrections to work, such as deleting errors. Be careful not to delete far too much and lose the work you did.

Overwrite

You saved a file yesterday and called it *essay*. You save a file today and also call it *essay*. Your new file overwrites the old file, which is lost.

Forget where you saved your work

Which disk did you use? What file name did you choose? If you don't remember, you may not see that work again.

A little bit of care will avoid mistakes like these. Data security helps you to avoid errors, and makes errors less serious.

Passwords

If you use a network at school you will have a network **password**. Don't tell anyone else your password – if someone asks you what it is, ask yourself why they want to know.

Don't use an obvious password (like your name). But make sure you choose a word which you can remember without writing it down.

As you type in your password it will not be displayed on the screen. This is so that nobody can look over your shoulder and see what it is.

Making backups

The most important thing to remember about data security is this: **make backups**. A backup is a second copy of a file, on another disk.

Everyone who uses computers professionally backs up all their work. That's because everyone makes mistakes, or has a hardware failure, at some time. Any work which is not backed up could be lost forever – disaster!

You will learn how to make copies of files on page 29. As soon as you know how, copy all your work files onto a spare floppy disk. Label the disk and put it somewhere safe. Then that work cannot be lost, no matter what problems occur in the classroom.

Save regularly

Many pupils only save their work when they stop at the end of a lesson. Don't wait that long. Supposing there is a system failure in the middle of your work?

It is easy to save your work with just a single click of the mouse. Every ten minutes or so, during the lesson, quickly save your file. Then, even if you do something disastrous, such as delete a page by accident, you can go back to the work you saved a few minutes before.

WHAT YOU HAVE TO DO

1. **Find out if the information on the computer at your school is backed up onto disk or tape. If it is, find out how often. Find out if the school backup can be used by pupils who lose or accidentally spoil their work.**

2. **Decide how often you are going to back up your own work. Where will you keep your backup disk?**

3. **Write some notes on the backup methods you have found out about.**

Keep your notes in your IT folder.

5. IT for everyone

How can you make sure everyone gets equal access to computers? On this last page in this section are some suggestions to make sure everyone in your class has a chance.

Equal access

Computers are for **everyone**. They make all types of work easier to complete. Everyone can learn how to use them. Computers can overcome difficulties that might have made work hard to do.

You should make sure that you don't feel excluded or prevented from making the most of computers. And you must also think about what you do yourself – are you making it difficult for anyone else?

Male and female

Everyone knows by now that both male and female pupils are just as good at using computers. Is the computer room at your school full of boys – or girls? It won't matter, just find yourself a place and start work. If anyone does try to tease you or exclude you, let a teacher know. Computer rooms are for *all* pupils.

Race and nationality

Everyone knows that pupils of all races and nationalities are just as good at using computers. An excellent feature of the Internet is that it lets you communicate with other young people from all over the world. One new invention is *translation software*, which can translate your sentences into other languages. This doesn't work very well yet, but it is sure to make it easier for people all over the world to share ideas and information.

Physical disability

Certain physical disabilities might make it harder for you to use the computer. These difficulties can be overcome. Special equipment is available to help disabled people make good use of the computer. Computers should make it easier for disabled people to complete tasks. For example, software is available which will read out the contents of a file instead of displaying it on the computer screen.

If you have a disability that makes it uncomfortable for you to use the computer, discuss this with your teacher. There may be some special equipment that can help you. It is your teacher's job to make sure that all pupils can make good use of the computers at school.

Computers at home

It's a fact of life: some people have computers at home and some don't. Some people have computers which are just the same as the ones at school, or perhaps even better. Others have older models or computers with different software. You should never feel disadvantaged just because you don't have access to a computer at home.

You should never be expected to complete work at home if that depends on using a computer. If you are set after-school work that involves using computers, you should be able to stay on at school after lessons and work using the computer facilities there.

If you feel you *are* being disadvantaged because you don't have a computer at home, talk to your teacher. You should have just as much chance as anyone else to become an expert.

Alternative input devices

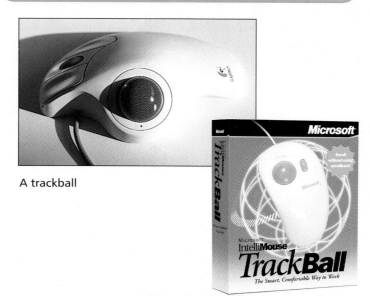

A trackball

A touch screen

On Target

Once you have worked through this introductory unit you should:

- be able to work safely and sensibly with the computer
- know the meaning of basic computer terms
- know how computer equipment is used
- ensure everyone gets proper access to computers.

WHAT YOU HAVE TO DO

1. Look back at the classroom rules you wrote on page 15. Suggest some changes and/or add more rules to allow equal access for all pupils.

2. Can you think of any circumstances that make it hard for you to complete computer work? Are you dyslexic for example? If you have any worries, then find a quiet time and mention them to your teacher.

I N T R O D U C T I O N

1

The User Interface

In this unit you will learn about the user interface. The user interface is what lets you work with the computer. It gives you the information you need and lets you give instructions to the machine.

On Target

In this unit you will learn about:

■ common features of the interface

■ what you will see on the screen

■ how to start up software packages

■ how to copy and delete work files.

These are skills and knowledge that will help you in the rest of your work. After you have worked through this unit, you will probably want to come back to it later on, for reference.

Windows

When you start up a software package it opens up in a **window** on the screen.

A window can be as large as the screen, or it can fill just a part of the screen.

You will learn more about windows over the next few pages.

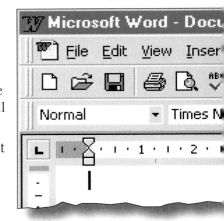

What is a Graphical User Interface?

Modern computers have a **Graphical User Interface**. That means the interface makes use of pictures, colours and shapes to help you use the computer.

A graphical user interface is sometimes jokingly called a WIMP system. W.I.M.P. stands for:

● Windows

● Icon

● Menu

● Pointer

These are the four key elements of a graphical user interface.

Alternative Interfaces

There are several different graphical interfaces. The interface used on **Apple** computers is slightly different to the **Microsoft** *Windows* system used on most other computers.
There are several different versions of Microsoft *Windows*, for example *Windows 3.x*, *Windows 95* and *Windows 98*.

If the interface used on your computer is slightly different to the one shown in the illustrations in this book, don't worry. Your computer will work in much the same way and you can use the same techniques.

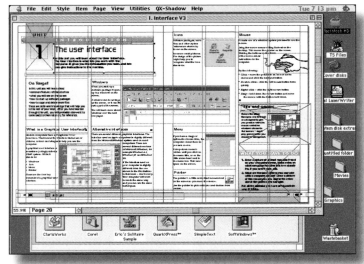

Load software p24   Windows features p26   Interface p30

Icons

Software packages, work files and other system features are shown by **icons** on the screen.

Icons are small pictures.

The design of the picture might help you to recognise what the icon stands for.

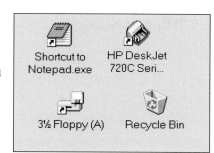

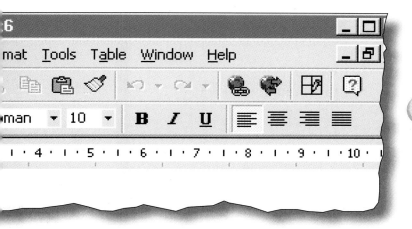

Menu

If you have a range of options to choose from, the computer shows them to you as a **menu**.

A drop-down menu is hidden until you click on the menu title, or on the little arrowhead next to the menu box. This saves space on the screen.

Pointer

The pointer is a little arrow that moves about on the screen as you move the mouse.

Use the pointer to pick out icons and choices from menus.

Mouse

To make use of a windows system you need to use the **mouse**.

Using the mouse means rolling it about on the desktop. This moves the pointer on the screen. Clicking the buttons on the front of the mouse sends instructions to the computer.

Try the following:
- **Click** – move the pointer to an icon or menu choice and click the left-hand button
- **Double-click** – click the left mouse button twice quickly
- **Right-click** – click the right mouse button
- **Drag** – hold down the mouse button and move the mouse with the button held down

Fun and Games

Games like *FreeCell* are designed to give you practise with the mouse and other windows elements. But beware – don't play games when you should be doing work.

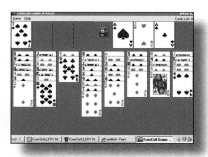

WHAT YOU HAVE TO DO

1. Draw a picture of at least one icon found on your computer screen. Make notes on what computer function this icon stands for. If you aren't sure, ask.

2. What are the main actions you can take with a computer mouse? Draw a picture of the mouse you use and write notes about the actions you can take.

Put all the material you have produced into your IT folder.

I. On the desktop

THE USER INTERFACE

On these pages you will be looking at the main features found on a typical desktop.

The desktop

The main screen of a typical graphical user interface is called the **desktop**. The desktop is what you see when you aren't using any particular package. The desktop gives you access to all the work files and software packages which are stored on your computer. On these pages you will be looking at the main features found on a typical desktop. The interface used here is **Microsoft *Windows 95***.

Key features

Your desktop will have certain key features:

- **icons**, which stand for:
  - storage areas
  - folders
  - files
- the **task bar**
- the **Start** button.

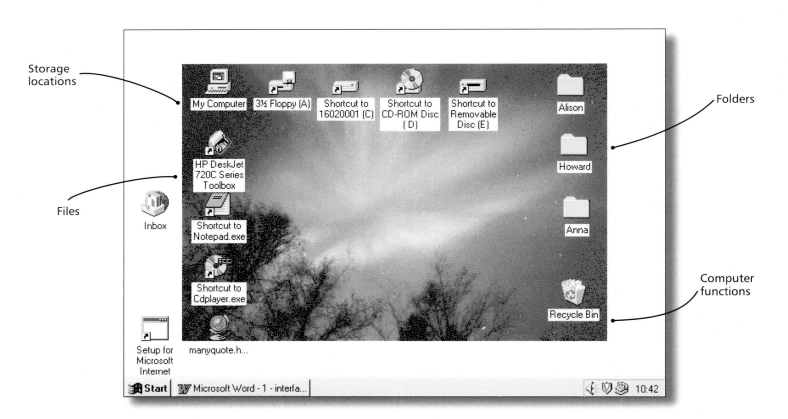

Every user arranges their desktop in a slightly different way. The desktop of your computer at home or at school may look quite different from this – but it will have the same basic features

Storage areas

To remind yourself of the types of storage which are available with a computer, look back at page 10.

On the desktop there are icons which stand for all the storage locations. If you double-click on one of these icons it will open as a window on the screen. You will see whatever is held in that storage location.

- Double-click on a storage location

A window will open. In the window you will see all the files that are stored in that location. Some of the files are collected into folders.

Folders

A storage location can hold literally hundreds of files. To make it easier to find the file you want they are arranged into **folders**.

- Double-click on a folder and it will open up as a window, showing you the files it holds

Folders can hold other folders.

You can have lots of windows open on the screen at once.

Files

When you open up storage locations and files you will find icons which stand for:

Work Files   Software Packages

On the next page you will learn more about starting up software packages and looking at work files.

Some interfaces are set up to show the contents of a window using large icons. In other cases you might see a list of icons, or a list of files. The information is the same. It is just shown in different ways.

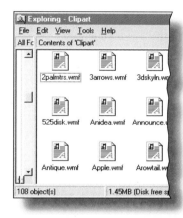
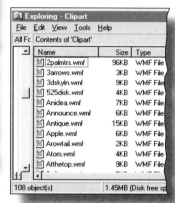

WHAT YOU HAVE TO DO

Investigate the desktop of the computer you use at school. Look at the various storage locations that are available to you and see what folders and files they contain.

- **What storage locations are accessible from the desktop?**

- **Do the windows you open show large icons, small icons, or lists of files?**

- **Are any file icons shown directly on the desktop itself?**

Write your answers to the questions above and put them into your IT folder.

2. Starting up

On this page you will find out how to start up a software package in three different ways:

- **click on a software package icon**
- **click on a work file icon**
- **use the Start button and Program menu.**

Starting the software

The desktop lets you start up software packages. You need to know:

- how to find a software package when you want to use it
- how to start it up in its own window so you can begin to work.

The methods shown on this page can be used to start up any of the software packages you will learn about in this book.

Different software packages are held in different locations on your computer system. Your teacher will tell you where to find the packages which you need to use for your course.

The next page has more information about the window which opens when you use a software package.

Software icons

Software packages are shown by **icons**. They may be shown on the desktop or in any of the folders and storage locations that you can reach from the desktop.

- Double-click on a software icon to start up the software package

 Backup.exe   Mspaint.exe   Scripter.exe

Work files

When you do work on the computer you have to save it as a **file**. Every file that you make has its own icon, in a folder, in the computer system.

 summary 1996-97.xls   summary 1997-98.xls

Double-click on a folder to see what files it contains

- Double-click on a work file

The computer will work out what software package you used to make the file. It will start up that software package and load your work, so you can continue with your task.

Double-click on a storage location to see what folders it contains

Double-click on a file to start it up

The Start button

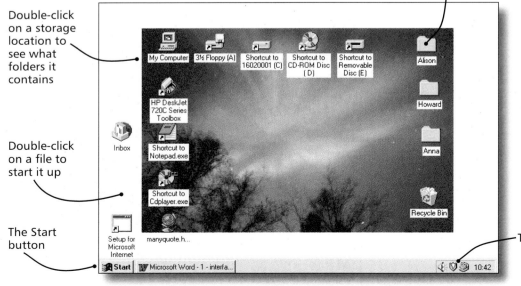

The task bar

Start up *Paint p34*

Start button

Another way to start up a software package is to use the **Start** button. This is in the bottom left-hand corner of the desktop.

- Click on the **Start** button and you will see the **Start** menu
- Click on the top word of the **Start** menu (Programs) to open the **Programs** menu

Programs menu

The programs menu lists all the software packages which are available on your computer. Some are shown as icons and some might be organised into folders. Your teacher will tell you if the package is stored in a folder.

- Click on the name of a package in the **Programs** menu to start it up
- Click on the folder icon to open it

Closing down

When you start up a software package it opens in its own window.

There is more information about software packages on the next page. For now all you need to know is how to shut one down.

Like all windows the software package window has a cross in the top right-hand corner.

- Click on the cross to close down the software package

Close down

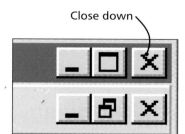

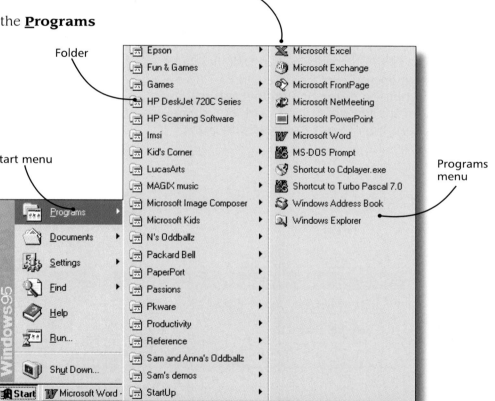

Folder

Icon

Start menu

Start button

Programs menu

The task bar

You can open more than one software package at once. All the packages which are open will be shown as buttons on the **task bar** at the very bottom of the desktop.

- Click on different buttons to swap between software packages

WHAT YOU HAVE TO DO

Practise starting up software packages using all three of these methods. Remember to close down all the packages once you have taken a look at them.

3. Opening the windows

Here you can learn about the key features of a software window. You need to be able to resize and close down windows.

Windows

When you open a software package you will see a **window** on the screen. It might fill the whole screen, or it might be smaller than the screen. Whatever software package you open, the window will have certain **key features**.

These features make it easier to learn a new Windows software package. It's like having a map when you explore a new place. If you know what the different symbols and colours stand for it's not difficult to work out where you are, or how to get to where you want to go.

Title bar

The **title bar** gives the name of the software package. If you have opened a working file then it also gives the name of the file.

Menu bar

You have seen that many windows menus are hidden. The **menu bar** has the titles of several menus.

● Click on any menu title to see the full menu

i The *Paint* window *p34*

Tool bar

On the last page you saw that icons are little pictures which stand for computer functions. The **tool bar** of a Windows package has icons. These stand for different actions you can take. For example this icon means *print out your work*.

● Click on the icon to use the tool

Working area

This is where your work will appear. If it is a graphics package, it is where the picture will be. If it is a word processing package, it is where the words will be and so on.

Scroll bar

It is quite likely that your work (for example a document) will be too large to fit into the window on the screen. Only part of it will be shown. To look at other parts of the document you use the **scroll bar**.

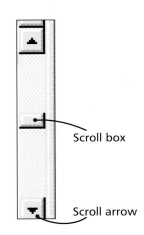

Scroll box

Scroll arrow

● Click above or below the scroll box to move up or down the document by one screen

● Click on the scroll arrow to move up and down by one line at a time

'This new idea of scrolling through text will never catch on.'

Resize buttons

The window can be as large as the screen or part-sized. It can also be reduced to the size of a small button on the task bar. The **resize** buttons will let you swap between these different sizes of window.

When the window is reduced in size, the resize buttons will look like this:

Shrink the whole window to a button

Expand the window to fill the whole screen

When the window is full size, the resize buttons will look like this:

Shrink the window to a button

Shrink the window to partial screen size

In some packages you will see two sets of buttons:

These buttons affect the working area only

These buttons affect the entire window

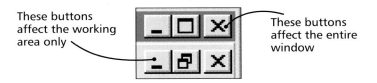

Closing down

In the top right-hand corner, next to the resize buttons, is the **close down** button.

● Click on this button to shut down the software package

If you close down the package your work will be lost unless it has been saved.

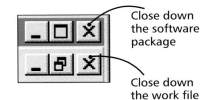

Close down the software package

Close down the work file

WHAT YOU HAVE TO DO

Start up one of the software packages on your computer at school. Find all the key features in the window. Open some of the menus and practise using the resize buttons. Close down the package.

4. In single file

The next step is to learn about:

- **moving and copying files**
- **deleting and restoring files.**

Looking after your files

Using the desktop you can carry out *tidying up* tasks, like:

- deleting work files that you don't want anymore
- copying files onto a backup disk.

The skills on this page will be most useful to you when you have built up a few work files. If you are only just starting out, you may not have created any files yet. If so, leave this page and remember to come back to it later.

My Computer

There is an icon on the desktop called *My Computer*.

- Double-click on this icon

My Computer

A window will open showing all the storage locations available from the computer.

You can open one of your work files from here but it's usually better to use *My Documents* or *My Work*.

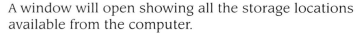

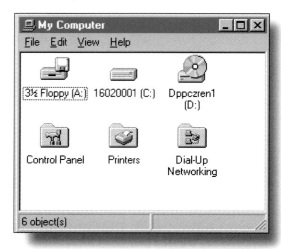

Locating files

To carry out the tasks on this page you must be able to see the icons of the files you want to work with.

- Double-click on the icon for the storage location where the file is stored. A window will open containing icons for files and folders
- Double-click on the folder where the file is stored. A window will open showing the contents of the folder

Sometimes folders contain other folders.

The file you want will be seen as an icon on the screen.

Dragging files

Most of the activities on this page involve moving file icons about on the desktop. To move a file icon you have to **drag** it.

Remember that to drag with the mouse you:

- **move** the pointer to the file icon
- **hold down** the mouse button
- keep the button **held down**
- **move** the pointer.

While the button is held down the file icon will be dragged along by the pointer.

When you get to the new location for the icon, let go of the mouse button. This will **drop** the icon in the new location.

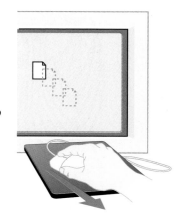

i File security *p20*

Moving

If you want to move a work file to a new place on the desktop just drag it from one place to another. For example:

- open the window where you know the file is
- open the window where you want the file to be
- drag the file icon from one window to another.

The file **Anna.doc** is moved from the folder **Old Files** to the folder **New Files**

Copying

If you drag a file icon to a new storage location, such as a floppy disk, then it won't be moved. It will be **copied**. The file will stay where it is, for example in your work folder. A new copy of the file will appear on the floppy disk.

You can use this method to copy your files and folders onto a backup disk.

The file **Anna.doc** is copied onto the floppy disk

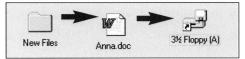

Recycle bin

This icon stands for the **recycle bin**. This is what you use to **delete** files which you don't want anymore.

If you drag a file icon into the recycle bin, the file is deleted from your computer system.

The file **Anna.doc** is deleted

Restore

You might delete a file, and then decide you made a mistake. If this happens, *don't worry!* You can **restore** files from the recycle bin. It's just like getting a piece of paper back out of a wastepaper basket.

You can simply drag the file icon back out of the bin and put it back where it belongs.

Be warned! You can't always restore files.

Beware!

If you drag a file from a floppy disk or another removable storage area into the recycle bin, it will completely disappear. You can't restore it.

If the recycle bin gets too full the computer will start to free up disk space by wiping out files which have been in the bin for a long time. So don't expect your files to sit in the recycle bin forever.

Disk to disk

Suppose you want to copy files from one floppy disk to another. Most modern computers only have room to hold one disk at a time. What can you do?

1. Put the disk with the files on it into the computer.
2. Open the floppy disk window on the desktop.
3. Drag the file icons from the disk onto the desktop – they will be copied onto your computer.
4. Close the floppy disk window and swap disks.
5. Drag the file icons from the desktop to the disk icon – they will be copied onto the new disk.
6. Delete the files from the desktop.

WHAT YOU HAVE TO DO

Practise these skills. If you have been working for a while and you have a number of work files, then take a look at the storage area where these files are held.

1. **Delete any files which you don't need anymore.**
2. **Make a copy of every file onto a floppy disk for backup.**
3. **Make sure the backup disk is labelled and put away somewhere safe.**

5. Which Windows?

Finally, if you are using a different interface from the one used in this book you should be aware of it. You will need to look out for any differences. However, it will not prevent you from following the examples given in this book.

Windows NT and Windows 98

The Windows interface that is used as an example in this book is called **Microsoft Windows 95**. But what if your computer uses a different interface?

If the computer you use at school or college runs a different system to *Windows 95* this is unlikely to be a problem. On this page there is a discussion of some of the different interfaces that are available.

Whatever interface you use, you should be able to follow the examples in this book.

Network Neighbourhood

The *Windows NT* desktop
The desktop looks much the same. You will see that as well as a *My Computer* icon there is a *Network Neighbourhood* icon

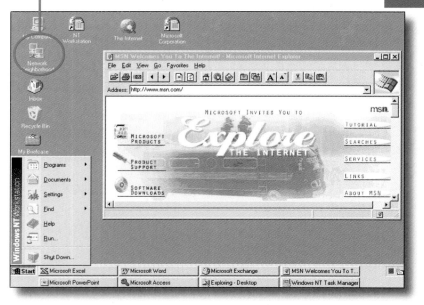

Windows 3.x

Before *Windows 95* there was a range of Windows products called *Windows 3.0, Windows 3.1*, etc. The shorthand for these systems is **Microsoft Windows 3.x**.

This interface doesn't have all the features which you will find in *Windows 95*. For example:

● there are no icons for work files, only software packages

● there is no Start button or task bar

● the windows are designed slightly differently

● to copy and delete files you use a special package called *File Manager*.

However, the similarities between these two packages are greater than the differences. You will be able to do most of the work in this book using an older Windows system.

Windows NT

A network joins a group of computers together. At the centre of the network is a **File Server**. You can save your work onto the file server and you can often get the software you need from the file server.

Microsoft *Windows NT* is designed to run over a network. It offers features to the people who run the network, letting them set up the system, add new users and manage the file server. But you don't need to worry about these features as you will never use them.

For you, as a user, *Windows NT* isn't too different from *Windows 95*.

i The desktop p22

Windows 98

The successor to *Windows 95* is **Microsoft *Windows 98***. It is basically the same in its main features but it offers some extra flexibility. Because of this flexibility the person who sets up the *Windows 98* system has a lot of choice about how it looks.

It might look more or less like *Windows 95*.

This interface looks a lot like *Windows 95* with folders like this one

The user has the choice of three interface styles

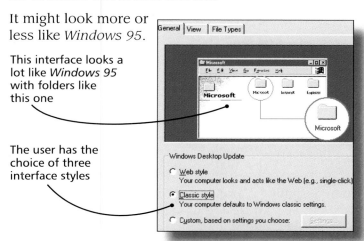

But *Windows 98* can also be set up to look more like the Internet. In other words, the software you use for your own computer looks like the software you use for the Internet.

Whatever you choose it will still include the task bar. It will also include the Start button menu.

You can use all the familiar features of *Windows 95* and follow the instructions in this book but look out for new features.

If you have the choice, avoid using Internet features at this stage. At least wait until you have completed Unit 7 which is all about Internet software.

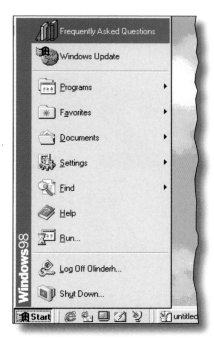

The Apple Macintosh

The graphical interface, with a desktop, was first developed by **Apple Macintosh**. The Macintosh desktop remains slightly different from the Windows system. Perhaps the biggest difference between the two is that the Apple mouse has only one button, so right-click is never used.

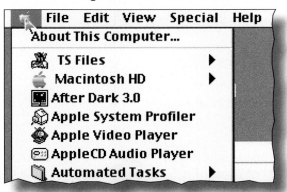

On Target

Now that you have worked through this unit you should know about:

- common features of the interface
- what you will see on the screen
- how to start up software packages
- how to copy and delete work files.

Remember you may need to come back to this unit again to remind yourself what to do.

WHAT YOU HAVE TO DO

1. **Make sure you know what interface you are using on the computer at school.**

2. **If you use a computer at home, check what interface is used on that computer.**

3. **Note down the interfaces you use.**

Keep your notes in your IT folder.

2 Graphics

Graphics use lines, shapes, colours, textures and patterns to show information.

Graphic images can be created using computers.

On Target

In this unit you will learn:

- how to use a mouse to move a pointer about on the screen
- the different tools available
- how to add text to a graphic
- how to select and combine features to create an image.

What are Graphics?

Lines, shapes, colours, textures and patterns are called **graphics**. Here are some examples of graphics:

- an illustration in a book
- the name of a company made into a logo or symbol
- the pattern on a piece of fabric
- an electrical wiring diagram
- a sketch you draw to show someone where your house is
- a cartoon in a newspaper.

Purpose and Audience

When designing a graphic you always need to keep its **purpose** and **audience** in mind.

The purpose of graphics is to show **information**. It should help make the information easy to understand.

Another purpose of a graphic is to make an **impression**. For example:

- bright colours suggest something fun and exciting
- straight lines or square shapes suggest something reliable and secure.

A company logo is an example of a graphic design. It tells you the name of the company in a visual way. It needs to be easy to understand and remember. It also needs to give an impression about the company – for example that it is exciting or reliable.

What impressions are these logos trying to give? How do they use graphics to give the right impression?

Graphics also need to be designed for a particular audience. The audience for a company logo is the people who might buy its products or services.

The same visual content can be shown in many different ways to suit the purpose and the audience for the image.

Below are graphic images of the same animal – a dog. Each one has been created for a different purpose and a different audience.

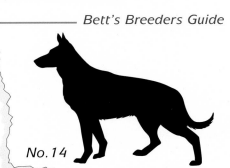

_____ Bett's Breeders Guide

No.14

To create a good graphic you need to think about its purpose and audience.

- What information needs to be provided?
- What impression should it give?
- Who is the information intended for?

You will find graphics very useful in your Art and Design and Technology lessons. You should be able to use graphics in Science and many other subjects too.

Computer Graphics

Computers can make it easier to create high quality graphics. Here are some of the reasons why:

- the computer will draw straight lines and perfect circles for you
- the computer will create clear, smooth colour effects
- you can delete your mistakes without making a mess
- you can easily try out many different effects to see which ones are best.

Over the following pages you will learn how to create high quality computer graphics.

WHAT YOU HAVE TO DO

1. **Look at the different examples of graphics on these two pages. For each one write down:**
   - **the purpose of the graphic**
   - **the audience for the graphic.**
2. **Make a collection of company logos. Explain the purpose and audience for each one.**

Keep your work in your IT folder.

I. Opening up

Graphics packages are designed to help you create images electronically.

In this unit you will need to use a tool bar and a mouse to create coloured shapes and lines on the computer screen.

Starting graphics

This page will help you to start creating graphics. You will find out:

- how to open the graphics package
- how a tool bar provides you with a set of features you can use
- how to select and combine features to create an image
- how a mouse is used to move a pointer about on the screen.

The package used here is **Microsoft** *Paint*. All graphics packages are fairly similar. You should be able to follow the instructions using any graphics package.

If you are already familiar with the basics of graphics packages, move on to the next page.

Opening the graphics package ■

The first thing you have to do is **open** the software package – that is load it from storage so that you can use it. Here is how to load Microsoft *Paint,* using the *Windows 95* software package.

1. Click on the **Start** button in the bottom left corner of the screen. You will see the Start menu

2. Pick the **Programs** option

3. You will see a list of all the programs available for you to use. Some are arranged into **folders**. The list is in alphabetical order. Find the **Accessories** folder. Click on it to open it up

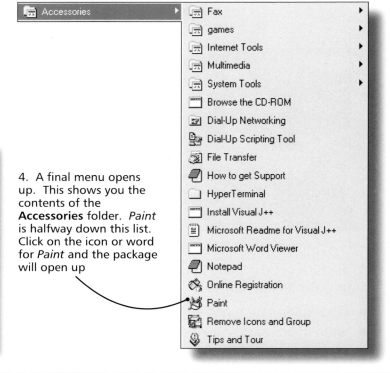

4. A final menu opens up. This shows you the contents of the **Accessories** folder. *Paint* is halfway down this list. Click on the icon or word for *Paint* and the package will open up

 Load software p24

Using the tools

- Find the tool bar on the screen. The icons on this bar stand for the different things you can do
- Experiment by clicking on the different tools and drawing in the working area of the screen

The little pictures on the tool bar are called **icons**. They stand for the tools that let you create different graphics on the screen

The **eraser** (rubber) lets you rub out the lines and shapes you have drawn

The **pencil** tool lets you draw thin freehand lines

For adding lettering

For adding straight lines

For adding squares and rectangles

For adding circles and ovals

1. Move the pointer to the tool bar and click on an icon to select a tool

2. Next, click on a colour

Keyboard tips

Find the **Shift** key on your keyboard.

If you press this key down as you draw shapes they will form perfect circles or squares.

3. Drag the mouse in the working area to create the type of graphic you have selected, in the colour you have selected

Using the mouse

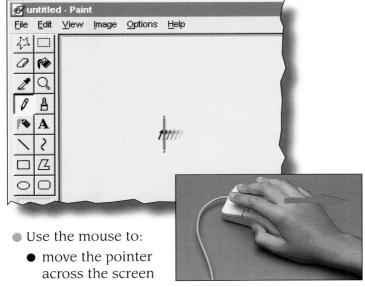

- Use the mouse to:
  - move the pointer across the screen
  - click on icons
  - drag lines across the screen

WHAT YOU HAVE TO DO

1. **Select the pencil or brush tool.**

2. **Hold down the mouse button and drag to create a freehand line. Try writing your own name on the screen.**

3. **Try writing your name again to see if you can improve it. It may be worth using the eraser tool to rub some or all of it out.**

4. **Enclose your signature with a coloured rectangular or oval shape.**

If you know how, save and/or print out your work. Keep your print-outs in your IT folder.

2. Save it or lose it

On this page you will learn:

- **how to save a graphics file**
- **how to bring back a file that you saved earlier.**

Saving your work

It is important that you remember to **save** your work. Make sure you do so before you switch off the computer or close down the graphics package. Unless you save your work you will lose it.

When you work on the computer your work is created in electronic form. If the electricity is turned off the work ceases to exist.

If you close down the software package without saving your work it will not remember what you have done.

When you save your work it is stored electronically. This means it is not lost when you stop work on the computer.

Keyboard tips

Instead of opening the **File** menu and picking **Save** you can hold down the **Control** key and press the **S** key.

File names

When you save your work you have to give it a **file name**. Make sure you pick a name that tells you what the file is about.

For example, on the last page, when you drew your signature, you could call the file:

My signature

or **Practice graphics file**

It's not a good idea to call files by your own name, or by just using a number (like *Graphics 1*). Later on you won't be able to remember what work the file has in it.

When you save your file the computer will probably add a dot and a three-letter file extension. So your file might become:

My signature.bmp

This three-letter extension helps the computer to know what type of file it is. Don't worry about this.

Save locations

The main storage locations are described on page 10.

The computer often identifies storage locations by a letter.

Drive **A**: the floppy disk drive

Drive **C**: the hard disk drive

Drive **D**: the CD-ROM drive (you can't use this to save work files)

The network might be drive **F** or **N**, or some other letter. Your teacher will tell you which.

 Storage *p10*

How to save

To save your file from a typical graphics package like Microsoft *Paint* you can use the menu system.

Click here

The *Save* window

When you select the **Save** option from the **File** menu you will see this window. You have to type a file name and select a storage location.

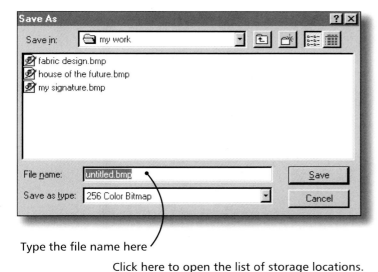

Type the file name here

Click here to open the list of storage locations.

Pick a storage location from this list

Save again

Once you have saved the work as a file you can use the same command at any time to save it again.

Select **Save** from the **File** menu, or press **Control** and **S**. The computer will save your work, using the same file name and storage location that you picked the first time you saved.

Each time the computer will save a slightly more completed piece of work. You won't have to use the *Save* window again.

It is a good idea to save like this every ten minutes or so, just in case something goes wrong.

Save as...

Sometimes you may want to change the name or the storage location for a file.

To save your work using a new file name, pick **Save As...** from the **File** menu.

You will see the *Save* window again. You can type in a new file name and/or storage location.

Printing

The other way to keep your work is to print it out. Your teacher will tell you when you are allowed to print out your work and what printer you should use.

To print your work:

- Open the **File** menu
- Pick the **Print...** option

You will see the **Print** window. Your teacher will give you instructions about how to use this window.

- Click on **OK** to start the print

Your work may go to a *Print Queue* with work from other people in your class. When it gets to the top of the queue it will be printed out. Collect your work from the printer when it is ready.

WHAT YOU HAVE TO DO

Save the signature file you made. Use a suitable storage location and file name.

3. Putting on the style

Who is your graphic going to be seen by?

How accurate will it need to be?

What decisions about brushes, line styles and shapes will you need to make?

Choosing the style of your graphics

On the last page you learned how to create a graphic with freehand **lines** and **shapes**. A graphics package can give you much more control over your designs. You can make choices about the style of the lines and shapes before you draw them.

By choosing the style of the graphic, you can make sure that your design is suitable for its purpose. If your graphic has to be eye-catching then you might choose wide lines. If your graphic has to be precise and accurate then you would choose narrow lines.

Make sure you are certain of the purpose of a graphic before you start to create it.

Sometimes you might want to make changes to the style of your graphic after it has been drawn. This is covered on pages 46–47.

Study the two different pictures of cars.

The one on the left might be used as the illustration for a children's book

The one on the right could be used to communicate precise information about the shape and size of the car

What type of brush?

- Click on the **brush** tool. You should be able to pick the shape and size of the brush you will use
- Practise with different brush shapes. See what type of line they draw

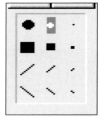 

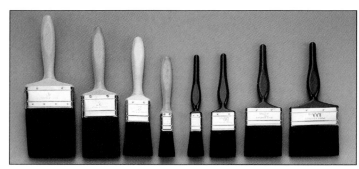

Line styles

- Select the **line** tool. You should be able to pick the width of the line you draw

Some packages let you put arrowheads on the lines, or draw dotted lines.

Filled shapes

● Select the **shape** tool. Draw some shapes. Shapes can be outline only, solid colour, or filled outline

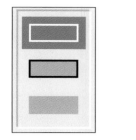
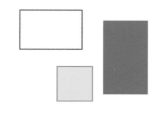

Foreground and background

Most graphics packages allow you to select two colours.

The **foreground** colour is used for all lines and outlines that make up the drawing.

The **background** colour is used when you draw a filled shape.

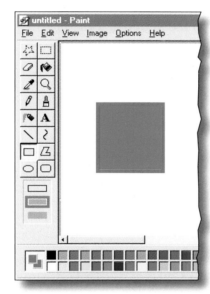

Look at the mouse. You should find that it has two buttons. Some have three. You usually use the left-hand button.

● Click on the colour palette with the **left** button to pick the **foreground** colour

● Click on the **right** button to pick the **background** colour

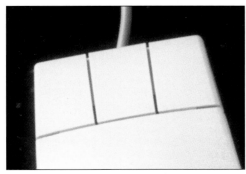

Undo

Most software packages include the **Undo** command. This is a very useful feature. It allows you to reverse the effect of the most recent change you made.

For example, if you delete part of a graphic and then wish you hadn't, you can use the **Undo** command. It will be as if you never deleted it. If you fill a shape with colour and don't like the effect, then give the **Undo** command – the picture will return to how it was before.

The **Undo** command is the first option on the **Edit** menu

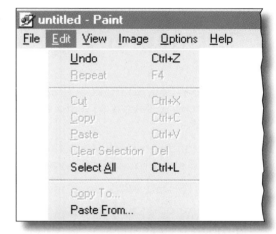

If you prefer, hold down the **Control** key and press the **Z** key.

4. An open and shut case

Next you will learn how to begin a completely new file and how to re-open a file you have saved.

Opening and closing files

You know how to make a graphics file. You know how to save it to a storage location, such as a disk.

On this page you will learn the remaining skills that you need to complete your work:

- how to start work on a new file
- how to open up a file you saved earlier
- how to close the software package when you stop work.

Try out the activities described on this page. These are skills you will use with all kinds of software packages.

IT at work

Many people are employed in the production of graphics of one type or another. For example:

- a draughtsman produces technical drawings for engineers and architects
- a graphic designer designs the appearance of documents and books
- a cartoonist produces funny pictures or adventure stories in picture form.

These days most work is done on a computer, so a high level of IT skill is essential.

Starting a new file

When you want to start a **new** picture, you choose **New** from the **File** menu. A new blank working area will appear.

Instead of using the file menu you can press the **Control** key and the letter **N**.

Many software packages allow you to work on several files at the same time. You can start up a new file without closing the old one down.

However, Microsoft *Paint* and some other simple packages are not like this. If you start a new file, the old one will close down. You have to make sure you save the old file first.

Exit from the package

When you **exit** from a package it is closed down. The software and all the work which you have created disappear from the computer's electronic 'brain'.

Click here to exit from the package

You can also use the **File** menu and **Exit** to exit from a package.

Another way is to press **Alt** and **F4**.

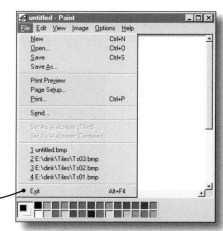

Click on **Exit**

File management p28

Warning message

If you start a new file or close down a package you will lose your work. That is unless you have given it a file name and saved it first.

If you have saved the work file but made changes since you last saved it, then you will lose the latest changes.

But don't worry – the computer will remind you. If you try to close down a file without saving it, you will see this warning message.

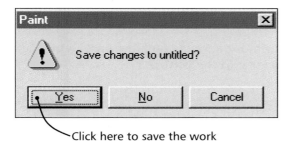

Click here to save the work

Opening an existing file

Opening a file means bringing it back from storage so that you can work on it again.

Open is an option in the **File** menu. Another method is to press **Control** and **O** (letter O, not the number 0).

When you give the **Open** command, with the menu or keyboard, you will see the **Open** window.

Click here to open the list of locations. Look through the list of locations and select the drive and folder you want

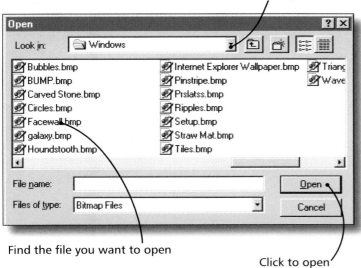

Find the file you want to open

Click to open

Opening from the desktop

As well as opening a file from inside a package you can find the right storage location on the desktop. When you open the folder you will see icons of all the work files in that folder.

● Find the icon of the file you want to open and double-click. The computer will start up the software package and open the file

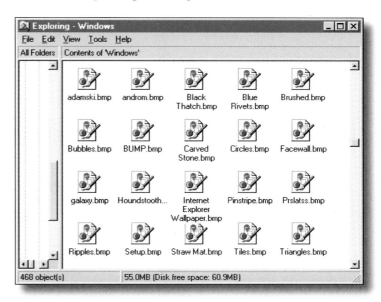

A disk full

Graphics files often take up a lot of space on a disk – much more than a text file. You may find that you are only able to save a few graphic files on your floppy disk. You may need to start a new disk.

WHAT YOU HAVE TO DO

Close down the graphics package if it is open. Make sure all your work is saved.

5. Any colour you like

Choosing the right colours for your design is important. Colour can communicate information and feelings.

This page will give you practice in adding colour to your computer graphic.

Using colour

Colour gives an image greater impact. In a painting, colour can express feeling. Good use of colour can make your graphics more useful, and attractive. Eye-catching designs depend on good colour choices. In maps, charts and diagrams, colour is used to convey information. Colour is also used to highlight important points.

On page 35 you learned how to use the colour palette. You should know how to pick a colour before you draw lines or shapes.

Here you will look at ways to add colour after you have created a design.

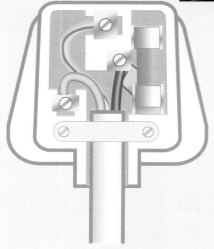

Filling a shape with colour

Most graphics packages include a tool which lets you pour colour into the picture.

● Draw a shape using ordinary lines

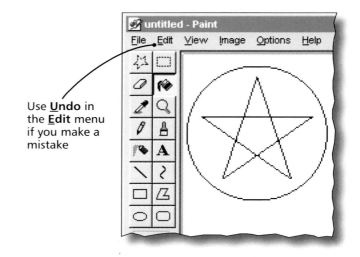

Use **Undo** in the **Edit** menu if you make a mistake

● Find the **Pour** tool. Add some colour to your shape

Here is an example of the same design after colour has been poured into it.

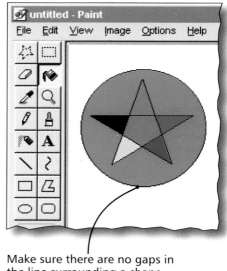

Make sure there are no gaps in the line surrounding a shape

Spray colour

A second way to add colour is to **spray** colour on. The tool you use may look like this:

This adds a fine pattern of light dots of colour. It is mainly used for eye-catching or artistic effects. Below is an example of a design using spray.

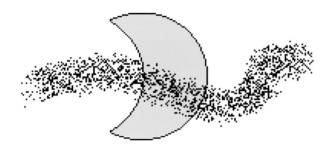

To re-create the design above:

- draw two overlapping ovals
- erase the unwanted sections of the ovals
- use colour fill in yellow
- use colour spray in black

- Experiment with the **Spray** tool to see what other graphic effects you can create

Know all about IT

If you *zoom in* to a picture created in a paint package you will see that it is made up of lots of small squares of colour.

Each square is called a *pixel* (short for *picture* or *pix elements*).

These are known as *bit-mapped* images. The mathematical position, colour and darkness of each pixel is remembered by the computer.

Use the **magnifying glass** tool to zoom in on a picture.

Place the magnify square anywhere on the picture. You will see that section enlarged on the screen.

IT at work

This outline shape could be used in a fabric design.

By using different colours a range of different effects can be easily produced.

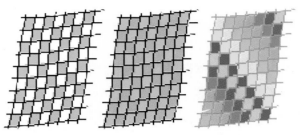

Textile designers often use graphics programs to help create new patterns. The computer enables them to experiment quickly with different pattern repeats and colour schemes.

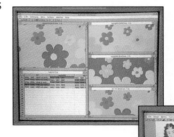

Using a 3D modelling package the design can then be draped onto a figure on screen. This will show exactly what the final garment will look like.

WHAT YOU HAVE TO DO

1. **Create a simple shape that could be used in a fabric design. Save the file.**

2. **Add different colours to the design. Produce several different versions.**

3. **Print one of your designs. If you don't have a colour printer you may have to print it in black and white. Check with your teacher first.**

4. **What sort of people might like the shapes and colours you have used?**

Keep your work in your IT folder.

6. Words and pictures

Most graphics need some text to go with them.
You will need to think about how the text looks.
How well does it fit with your graphic?

Adding text to your graphics

Most graphics need words as well as images. Letters and numbers can be added using the keyboard.

Text can be used for:

- titles
- headings
- labels
- instructions
- design elements.

You can also add information such as your name and the date.

You will find it easy to add text to a graphic. Learn how to alter the size and style of the text.

The size and style of text is called the **font**. Learn how to make changes to the font. This will improve the appearance of the text you add to your graphics.

Would you believe IT!

How well does the text fit the graphic?

The text tool

- Find the **text box** tool
- Create a box on the screen

Click on this tool to enter text into the graphic

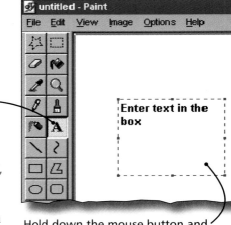

Enter text in the box

Hold down the mouse button and drag to draw this text box on the screen

- After you have drawn the text box, type letters and other characters. They will appear in the text box

Making changes

- Check your typing carefully. While the text box is open you can:
  - type new text
  - delete any mistakes
  - change the size of the text box

As soon as you click anywhere else on the screen the text box disappears. The text remains on the screen but you can't make any more changes. If the text is wrong, delete it and start again.

Changing the size of the text box

The larger dots on the text box are called **re-sizing handles**.

- Drag these handles to change the size and shape of the text box

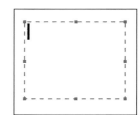

 Merging pictures and text *p70*

Choosing fonts

The **font** means the size and style of the letters.

Here are some examples of font shown in different sizes:

Helvetica 10 point

Times New Roman 14 point

Handel Gothic 18 point

Point is a measure of size. Most books and magazines use 10, 11 or 12 point letters for the text. Headings are usually between 14 and 20 point.

Here is an example of a tool bar which lets you pick the font:

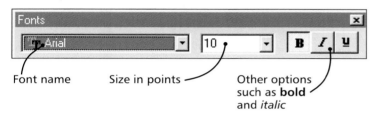

Font name   Size in points   Other options
                                 such as **bold**
                                 and *italic*

The list of font names and sizes is stored in a **drop down menu**.

In some packages you won't see the font tool bar. In Microsoft *Paint* you have to click inside the text box with the **right** mouse button to open this tool bar.

- To open the drop down menu, click on the little arrowhead. Then pick the font you want from the list

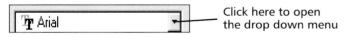

Click here to open
the drop down menu

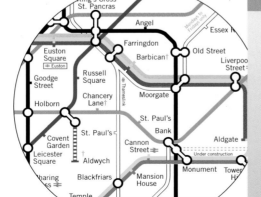

Special text fx

More complicated graphics packages include a range of tools which enable you to create some unusual lettering. These can be used for special headings.

Below are some examples. Find out if your school has a graphics package that can create these effects.

WHAT YOU HAVE TO DO

1. **Look back at the graphics files you created on the computer during this unit. Add suitable titles and your name and class.**

2. **Use the computer to draw a simple map of part of your school. Make it look similar to the London Underground map. Use coloured lines for corridors and squares and circles to show classrooms.**

Remember to save and/or print your work. Keep your work in your IT folder.

7. Self-selection

Once a graphic has been created it is easy to make changes to it. The way you do this depends on the type of software package you are using.

Selecting parts of the graphic

So far you have added new items and colours one by one to create an image. On this page you will learn how to select the items and make changes to them.

Once you have selected part of the image you can:

- delete it
- move it to another part of the drawing
- make copies of it
- change its size or shape
- flip or rotate it.

There are two types of graphics package. One is called **bitmap**. The other is called **vector**. These two types of package work in different ways. For example, the way you make selections is different.

Microsoft *Paint* is a good example of a bitmap package.

CorelDRAW is a popular drawing package that uses vector graphics.

Graphics packages that are included as part of word processing software (such as Microsoft *Word*) tend to use vector graphics.

Bitmap packages

In a **bitmap** package the computer stores the position and colour of all the dots that make up the image. When you select part of a bitmap image, you select all the dots inside an area of the screen.

- Use the selection tool to draw a line around the *area* that you want to select

This tool lets you select a regular rectangular area

This tool lets you select an irregular area

- Draw a line round an area with the *irregular* shape tool, *or*
- Drag with the *regular* shape tool to select a rectangle of screen

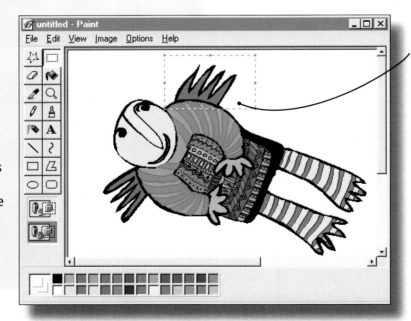

In this **bitmap** package the area of screen with the angel's wing has been selected using the regular shape tool

Vector packages

In a **vector** package the computer stores all the lines and shapes that make up the image.

When you select part of a vector image you select a complete line or shape.

- Click on the *shape* you want to select with the mouse pointer

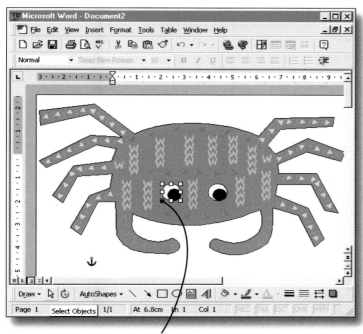

In this vector package, the crab's eye has been selected

You can make changes to the selected item without changing the rest of the picture.

Deleting a selected item

When you have selected an *area* of the screen (bitmap packages) or a *shape* (vector packages), you can delete it. Press the **Delete** key on your keyboard to remove the item you have selected.

Hardware

Using a keyboard and mouse is not the only way to get images onto the computer screen. Find out if your school has a **Graphics Tablet**. It comes with a special pen. You can draw on screen much more accurately with a tablet and pen than with a mouse.

Another possibility is to use a scanner. A scanner is a bit like a fax machine. Lines are changed into electronic signals. Drawings or photographs can be scanned in and changed in the computer.

WHAT YOU HAVE TO DO

1. **Find out if you are using a bitmap or a vector package. Do you have access to both types of packages? What are they called?**

2. **Create a simple logo made up from your initials. Use either a bitmap or a vector package, or ideally both. What are the advantages and disadvantages of each type of package for creating logos?**

Remember to save and/or print your work. Keep your work in your IT folder.

8. On the move

You now know how to select and delete part of a graphic. On the last page of this unit you will explore some of the other actions you can carry out with a selected part of a picture.

Cut, copy and paste

In this section you will learn how to

■ move   ■ copy   ■ cut   ■ paste

a selected part of a graphic.

When you **move** part of a graphic you can still see it on the screen, but in a new place.

When you **copy** part of a graphic it remains on the screen. The computer stores a copy of it in an area of electronic memory called the **clipboard**.

When you **cut** part of a graphic it disappears from the screen, as if it has been deleted, but the computer keeps a copy in the **clipboard**.

When you **paste**, whatever is stored in the clipboard is inserted back into the picture.

As an example you will see how the design on this page can be transformed using move, cut, copy and paste.

Select

Before you can move, cut or copy an item you have to **select** it. To remind yourself how to select parts of a graphic, look back to page 46.

In this picture, part of a graphic has been selected with the **irregular** shape tool.

Move

To **move** part of a picture to a new place:

● Select the item or area of the screen
● Hold down the mouse button and drag the item across the screen

Cut

To **cut** part of a picture:

● Select the item or area
● Pick **Cut** from the **Edit** menu (or use the keyboard shortcut **Control** + **X**)

The item disappears from the picture. But this is *not the same as delete* because the item is stored in the clipboard. You can't see it but it is there. It can be pasted.

 i Cut and paste between packages *p70*

Paste

To **paste** an item from memory into a picture:

- Pick **Paste** from the **Edit** menu (or use the keyboard shortcut `Control` + `V`)

You may have to **drag** the item to the place where you want it to appear.

Copy and paste

Instead of cutting an item to put it into the clipboard you can **copy** it. Copy means that the item stays on the screen and it is stored in the clipboard.

To **copy** part of a picture:

- Select the item or area

- Pick **Copy** from the **Edit** menu (or use the keyboard shortcut `Control` + `C`)

Once an item has been copied (or cut) into the clipboard you can **paste** it as often as you like. You can put the same item into your picture over and over again.

On Target

In this unit you should have learned:

- how to use a mouse to move a pointer about on the screen
- the different tools available
- how to add text to a graphic
- how to select and combine features to create an image.

IT at work

In company reports, designers often use graphics to make numerical information easy to understand.

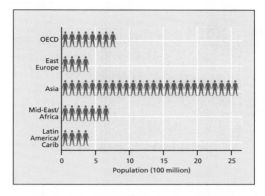

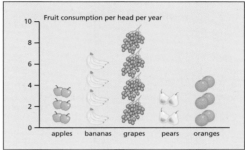

Keyboard tips

There are keyboard shortcuts you can use instead of opening the **Edit** menu.

Cut	`Control` + `X`
Copy	`Control` + `C`
Paste	`Control` + `V`

WHAT YOU HAVE TO DO

1. On page 43 you created a shape for a fabric design. Re-open the file you used to do this. Select the image and use cut and paste to make a repeat pattern design.

2. Show a range of designs with different combinations of colours.

Remember to save and/or print your work. Keep your work in your IT folder.

3

Word Processing

**This unit is all about working with words.
Word processing software helps makes it easier and
quicker to draft texts, check and correct them, and print
them out really neatly.**

On Target

In this unit you will learn how to use word processing software to:

- type documents
- find and correct errors
- change the appearance of the text and layout
- save and print the work.

By the time you have finished you should be happy about using word processing to prepare all your text documents. On this page you will look at some of the advantages of using a word processor to:

- remove the errors from your work
- make your documents easier to read
- give exactly the impression that you want.

Advantages

Word processors have many advantages over the typewriter. They get things done more quickly and more accurately. You can make changes more easily. Spelling and grammar can be checked. The file can be kept on the computer for later reference, or sent in seconds to anywhere in the world using the Internet.

Putting It In Your Own Words

A lot of the work you have to do at school involves putting words down on paper. You write essays, reports and other documents.

But what makes a good document?

- Accuracy
- Clarity
- Suitability

Accuracy

The first important feature of text documents is that they are accurate – free of mistakes. Word processing software will let you:

- *find errors* such as spelling mistakes
- *correct any mistakes* without untidy crossing out.

Making changes to a computer file is called **editing**.

- Learn about finding and correcting mistakes on page 60.

Clarity

As well as being free from errors your document should be clear and easy to read. Documents which are broken up into paragraphs are easier to read than documents that are just one long block of text. Headings and sub-headings make your document even easier to understand.

You should also make sure that you don't use colours and styles of text which are hard to read.

- Learn about text style and colour on pages 56–59.
- Learn about text layout on page 62.

Suitability

Finally, your document must make the right impression. Think about:

- the **purpose** of your document – *what* is it for?
- the **audience** for your document – *who* is going to read it?
- the **impact** of the document – *what impression* do you want to give?

For example:

If the purpose of the document is to attract attention then the text should be bright and bold.

If the audience for the document is made up of young children then the text should be large and simple.

Spot digs.
Spot digs and digs.
Spot digs and digs and digs in the sand.

If you are writing a birthday card then you want to give an impression that is friendly and personal. Word processing wouldn't be suitable for this type of document.

Getting IT Right in...

English

Here is an example of how you can use text formatting to improve the work you do at school.

A pupil wrote this about his hobby of keeping pet lizards:

> There are many species of lizard that may be available in a local pet store. The beginner should choose the species carefully because some are much easier to look after than others. Among the easy species are: Leopard Geckos, Anoles, Skinks and Bearded Dragons. More difficult Lizards are Day Geckos, Iguanas and Water Dragons. The most difficult lizards to look after are Chameleons, Monitors and Tegus and no beginner should choose one of these species.

By reformatting his text he changed it to look like this:

> **Lizard Species**
>
> There are many species of lizard that may be available in a local pet store. The beginner should choose the species carefully because some are much easier to look after than others. I have divided species of lizard into easy, difficult and impossible for beginners.
>
> | *Easy* | *Difficult* | *Impossible* |
> | --- | --- | --- |
> | Leopard Gecko | Day Gecko | Chameleon |
> | Anole | Iguana | Monitor |
> | Skink | Water Dragon | Tegu |
> | Bearded Dragon | | |

These simple changes have made the text much more interesting and easy to read, though the basic information has not been changed.

WHAT YOU HAVE TO DO

Collect examples of text which use different print styles, sizes and colours. On your own, or as a class, try to answer these questions.

1. **What is the purpose of this document?**

2. **Who is the audience for this document?**

3. **What impression is the document trying to give?**

4. **What information is being communicated?**

I. On keyboards

To begin with you will look at one of the most basic skills of word processing – typing in words using the keyboard.

Working with words

You need to:

- know your way round a word processing package
- be able to use the main features of the screen
- know how to use the keyboard to enter text.

The window ■

Like any other software package the word processor opens up into its own window. An example is shown below. See if you can identify:

- the title bar
- the menu bar
- the tool bar
- the resize buttons
- the scroll bar
- the working area.

If you can't identify any of these items look back at page 26.

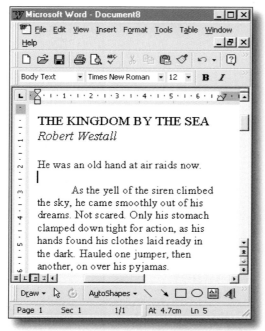

The cursor ■

The cursor is a flashing black line that can be seen on the word processing screen. When you type new text it appears at the cursor. Any other changes like deleting text also take place at the point marked by the cursor.

and |

The text pointer ■

When you move the mouse pointer onto the part of the screen where the words can be seen, it changes. It no longer looks like an arrow, it looks something like this:

The text pointer

- Move the text pointer to a place in the text and click with the mouse button

The cursor will move to that place.

Moving the cursor ■

If you look back over something you have typed you might see a mistake you want to delete. Or, you might want to add a new word, right in the middle of your work.

What you need to do is move the cursor to the place where you want to make the change.

There are two ways to move the cursor:

- use the mouse to move the text pointer to where you want the cursor to be and click the mouse button
- use the arrow keys on the keyboard to move the cursor up and down or left and right.

Using the keyboard

When you are using a word processing package your main tool is the keyboard. Not all keyboards look exactly the same. However, you should be able to find each key mentioned here on the keyboard you use at school.

At first you will find typing is slower than writing but, if you practise, you can quickly pick up speed.

Enter

The **Enter** key (sometimes called the **Return** key) is the largest key on the keyboard. When you press this key the cursor moves down to the next line. This is called a **line break**.

You don't need to press the **Enter** key when you are typing in normal text. The computer will split up the text into lines for you.

Only press the **Enter** key when you want a line to finish early, for example at the end of a paragraph.

Backspace

The **Backspace** key deletes letters backwards from the cursor.

Shift

If you hold down the **Shift** key as you type a letter you get a capital.

If you hold down the **Shift** key while you press one of the other keys you get the symbol which appears at the top of the key.

- Press the **Shift** key and **5** to type %

Caps lock

If you press the **Caps Lock** key you lock the keyboard to capital letters.

Sometimes there is a light on the keyboard that comes on when this happens. Press the button again to turn the caps lock off.

Insert and overtype

Usually when you type new letters they are **inserted** into the text at the cursor.

But if you switch to **overtype** then the letters will be *typed over* the text that is there already, rubbing it out.

- Press the **Insert** key to swap between **insert** and **overtype**

Many packages display a little message at the bottom of the screen to remind you if you are in overtype mode.

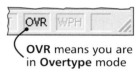

OVR means you are in **Overtype** mode

Number lock

The arrow keys move the cursor around in the text.

Some keyboards have separate arrow keys. On some keyboards the arrow keys are combined with number keys.

To use these as arrow keys you must make sure the **Number Lock** (Num Lock) light is **off**. To turn it off, press the **Num Lock** key.

WHAT YOU HAVE TO DO

1. Find out which word processing package you are going to use and how to start it up.

2. Study the keyboard of your computer and find all the keys mentioned on this page.

3. Type up the piece shown in the word processing window on page 52. Use the word processing tools to make sure your copy is accurate.

2. Save it. Print it. Close it.

This page covers all the skills you need to work with document files. You will learn how to:

- **start new documents**
- **save files you have created and print out your work**
- **close down a file when it is finished.**

Save, print and close your document

You have learned how to type up a word processed document, such as a school essay. But unless you learn how to print it out you can't hand it in. And unless you learn how to save it you will lose it when you stop work for the day.

To do these different tasks you will make use of icons on the tool bar. The tool bar of a word processing package is at the top of the window, underneath the menu bar. Each icon on the tool bar stands for a different action.

The package used here is **Microsoft *Word***.

In any typical word processing package the icons you need will look something like this. These are found in the top left hand corner of the word processing window.

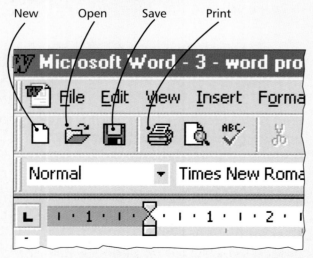

The top left corner of the word processing package

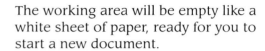

New

If you want to start a new blank document then click on this icon:

The working area will be empty like a white sheet of paper, ready for you to start a new document.

Open

Open means *bring back a file from storage*. The **Open** icon on the tool bar looks like this:

When you click on this icon the *Open* window will appear and you can pick which file you want to open.

To remind yourself how to pick the file you want, look on page 28.

Save

The **Save** icon on the tool bar looks like this:

Click on this icon to save your document for the first time. The *Save* window will appear and you can pick a **storage location** and a **file name**.

You can click on this icon at any time while you work. The document will save again, using the same file name and location as before.

Remember: don't wait until the end of the lesson to save your file. Keep saving it from time to time as you do your work. This is the safest way.

If you want to remind yourself about how to save a file then look on page 36.

Save as...

If you want to change the file name or the location you use to store the file then you should pick **Save As...** from the **File** menu.

Print

The **Print** icon on your tool bar looks like this:

Click on this icon to start a standard print of your document. Always check with your teacher first before you print.

You may want to change some of your print options, such as which printer you use. Go to **File**, and then click on **Print...** to open up the *Print* window.

If you need to remind yourself about printing then look on page 37.

Close and exit

When you have finished work, and saved your document, you can decide to:

- close the work file but keep the software package on screen to do more work
- exit from the software package and stop work completely.

Remember that the X in the top corner of a software window lets you close the window. In a typical word processing package there are two Xs which let you choose between these two options:

- the top X lets you close down the whole package
- the lower X lets you close the document but keep the package open.

The file menu

Most of the options you have learned about on this page are also found in the **File** menu. You can pick them from this menu if you don't want to use the icons on the tool bar.

The file menu

IT at work

Almost all businesses create paperwork of one kind or another:

- people in business send letters to each other
- companies produce publicity material
- people who work together circulate memos with important information
- when a task is complete you often produce a report on what you have done.

Nowadays all of this paperwork is produced using a word processor.

There are some jobs that mainly involve typing up documents. For a secretary, word processing might be a major part of the job. But in most jobs nowadays you are expected to have a general working knowledge of how to type up a document on a computer.

WHAT YOU HAVE TO DO

1. **Look at the tool bar of your word processing package. Try to identify the icons which stand for each of the actions described on this page.**

2. **Open the File menu of your word processing package. Find all the options mentioned on this page.**

3. Putting on the style (I)

Next you will learn about some of the text formats that you can use.

Changing the style

So far you have learned how to enter plain text. But there are other choices for how the text can look. Your documents can include text of different styles and sizes. The text doesn't have to be plain black on white. Different styles of text are called **text formats**.

By using different text formats you can make your documents easier and clearer to read. You can also improve the impact of the documents.

The tool bar

The tool bar has icons which let you pick all the different text formats.

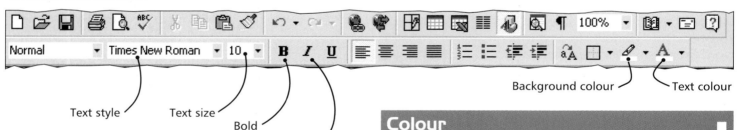

Text style | Text size | Bold | Italic

Pick a format

To pick a format for your text:

● click on the tool bar icon
● type the words
● click on the same icon to turn the format off.

Toggles

All the text format tools shown on this page are **toggles**. That means that you use the same command to switch them on and off.

If you click an icon to switch **on** a text format, you click the same icon to switch it **off** again.

Bold and italic

Bold text is **darker** than normal.

Italic text *leans over* to the side.

Both of these styles can be used to emphasise headings and important words.

These tool bar icons are **toggles** for **bold** and *italic*

Colour

These icons let you pick the **colour** for the text and the text background.

Here they are set to pick white text on a blue background. It would **appear like this**. But you can pick from a range of colours by clicking on the arrowhead next to the icon.

Click on this arrow to see the range of colour choices

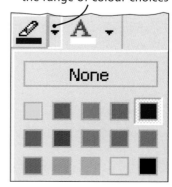

None

i   Graphic style *p38*   More style features *p58*

Text sizes

As you learned in Unit 2 about Graphics, text size is measured in **points**.

10 point is small text.

14 point is large text.

20 point is enormous text.

Click here to open the list of sizes

10
8
9
10
11
12
14
16
18
20
22
24
26

This part of the tool bar is used to pick text size. As with colour, click on the arrowhead to see a list of choices.

Fonts

Font means style of text.

There are hundreds of fonts. Some are fancy, some are plain, some are serious and some are very silly.

- Click to open the list of fonts and use the scroll bar to move up and down the list
- Try out a few fonts until you find the one you like

Times New Roman

- **T** SymbolProp BT
- **T** Tahoma
- **T** Technical
- **T** Tempus Sans ITC
- **T** Times New Roman
- **T** Times New Roman MT Extra Bold
- **T** Times New Roman Special G1
- **T** Times New Roman Special G2
- **T** Trebuchet MS
- **T** VAGRounded BT
- **T** Verdana
- **T** Viner Hand ITC

Helvetica
ABCDEFGHIJKLMNOPQRSTUVWXYZabcdefghij
klmnopqrstuvwxyz123456789

Brush
ABCDEFGHIJKLMNOPQRSTUVWXYZabcdefghijklmnopqrst
uvwxyz123456789

Times New Roman
ABCDEFGHIJKLMNOPQRSTUVWXYZabcdefghij
klmnopqrstuvwxyz123456789

Oz Handicraft
ABCDEFGHIJKLMNOPQRSTUVWXYZabcdefghijklmnopqrstuvwxyz123456789

Bullet points

To make a list easier to read you can put each item on a different line and add **bullet points**. Bullet points are usually small black circles.

- To enter items as a bulleted list press **Enter** to start a new line and click on this icon:

Now every time you press **Enter** you will get a new bullet point.

- Click on the same icon to stop adding bullet points

Numbers

Sometimes instead of bullet points you want to number a list. For example if you are writing a list of answers to questions you might want each answer to start with a number.

The icon to create a numbered list looks like this:

Use it in just the same way as the bullet points icon.

WHAT YOU HAVE TO DO

Earlier you collected examples of text and made notes on how text style was used to add impact (see page 51).

1. **Take one of the text samples from your collection and type it in yourself. If the sample is long then only type in the first part of the text.**

   - **Copy the words and choose text formats from those available in your word processing package.**
   - **Pick the style size and colour of the text.**
   - **Add bullet points or a numbered list if you wish.**

   Save and print the work.

2. **Write notes comparing your version of the text with the sample you copied. How have you added impact to the document?**

4. Putting on the style (2)

On this page you will discover how to swap between different text formatting styles. You need to try out different styles until you find the one you think works best.

Editing a document

After a document has been created you can go back to it and make changes. You can change the text itself, by deleting and inserting words and letters. You can also change the text formats used, for example the colour of the text or the use of **bold**.

Delete and insert ■

On page 52 you learned how to move the cursor around in a piece of text, using the arrow keys or the mouse.

● If you move the cursor to a place in the text then you can add new typing at the cursor.
● You can also delete using the **Backspace** key.

Use these techniques to make changes to the text. You can correct errors, or make improvements.

Select a block of text ■

You can select a block of text using the mouse.

● Move the text pointer to the start of the block of text.
● Hold down the mouse button and *drag* the mouse pointer to the end of the block of text.
● Release the mouse button.

All the selected area of text will be highlighted, like this, **black on white** .

If you press the **Backspace** key then the whole block of text will be deleted.

Change the format ■

You can also change the format of the selected block of text.

You have learned which icons on the tool bar let you choose text formats like:

● text style
● text colour
● italic
● numbered list
● text size
● bold
● bulleted list.

If you can't remember the icons which let you choose these formats then look back to page 56.

You can change the format for a selected block of text using these same tool bar icons. Here is how you do it:

● Select the block of text
● Click on the tool bar icon

All the selected block of text will change to the format you picked.

Remove format ■

Remember the text format tools are **toggles**. The same icon is used to switch the format on and off.

Remove a format from a block of text by doing this:

● Select the block of text
● Click on the tool bar icon

This will switch the format off.

Add headings and sub-headings ■

A good way to improve a piece of text is to add headings and sub-headings.

To add a heading to a piece of text:

● Move the cursor to the place where you want the heading to be
● Press **Enter** once or twice to insert empty lines
● Type the text of the heading

Remember to pick suitable text formats for headings.

● Make the main heading the largest. **Abc**
● Sub-headings should be smaller. **Abc**
● Less important headings could be lower case italic or bold. **Abc**

Remember that bold letters look bigger, so may not need to be so large.

Try to avoid using all capital letters in headings. Using capital letters is a bit like **SHOUTING**.

Brightwell School
Charity Week
Tuck Shop Menu
Carrot Cake 45p
Chocolate Cookies 20p
Cinnamon Squares 20p
Truffle Treats 35p
Date and Walnut Bars 30p
Room 101
10.45 – 11.15
12.00 – 1.15
Every day this week.

Undo ■

Undo reverses the last command you gave. If you are making changes to a document and you realise you have made the wrong change, just use **Undo** to go back to how it was before.

● To undo the last action you took, click on this icon

For instance, suppose you selected and deleted a big block of text. Then you discover – horror – that you shouldn't have deleted it, or that you deleted too much. Never mind. Click on the **Undo** icon and the text will come back just as it was.

In some packages you can undo more than one previous action. Just click the **Undo** icon over and over again and it will undo one command after another.

Making an impression ■

In order to raise money for charity a class has been given permission to make and sell cakes at break time. This is the text of their menu and price list:

Brightwell School, Charity Week, Tuck Shop Menu

Carrot Cake 45p Chocolate Cookies 20p

Cinnamon Squares 20p Truffle Treats 35p

Date and Walnut Bars 30p Room 101

10.45 – 11.15 12.00 – 1.15 Every day this week.

The pupils decided to improve the appearance of the text. Their first effort is on the left.

It's quite bright and colourful, but the different choices don't go together very well. Yellow was a poor choice for the time and place – this important information is hard to read.

Here is the final version. Fewer styles have been used and the colours are better chosen.

Brightwell School
Charity Week
Tuck Shop Menu
Carrot Cake 45p
Chocolate Cookies 20p
Cinnamon Squares 20p
Truffle Treats 35p
Date and Walnut Bars 30p
Room 101
10.45 – 11.15, 12.00 – 1.15
Every day this week

WHAT YOU HAVE TO DO

On the previous page you copied a sample of text and made your own choices of text format. Open this document.

1. **Select blocks of text and change the fonts used.**

2. **Change the colours, styles, sizes and any other features you like.**

3. **Print out the new file and save it using a new file name.**

4. **Write notes comparing your two files. Which text formats do you think are most successful?**

5. Spelling test

On this page you will learn how to use your word processing package to help you achieve perfect spelling in all your work.

Checking your spelling

Does your spelling let you down?

Are you good at spelling, but sometimes make careless mistakes?

Do you sometimes have to look up spellings in the dictionary?

Whatever your spelling is like, a word processing package can help you.   A modern word processor will:

- find spelling mistakes
- suggest the correct spelling
- make the change for you.

IT at work

Not so long ago our daily newspapers were printed from metal letters. This was called *letterpress.* Today they are produced electronically.

A reporter types up a story in a word processing package. The text is then placed in a desktop publishing package. This allows columns of text and pictures to be moved around quickly and easily on screen. It is easy to make last-minute changes as new stories break.

How does it work?

The computer stores a list of words. It checks every word you type against this list. If it finds a word which is not on the list it picks this out as a spelling mistake.

Spell check window

This icon on the tool bar starts the **spell check** for your document.

Once you start the spell check the computer will pick out every mistake it finds, showing a window like this:

This is the spelling mistake the spell check found

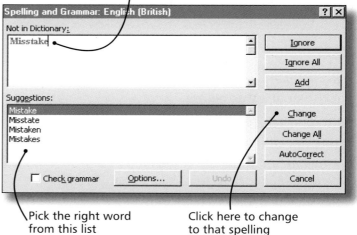

Pick the right word from this list

Click here to change to that spelling

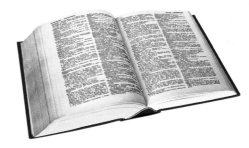

Marking spelling mistakes ■

Some word processing packages pick out the spelling mistakes as you type. They often mark them with a wiggly red line like this:

There is a spelling misstake in this document

If you know the right spelling just retype the word. But if you aren't certain, then **right-click** on the word. That means click with the right-hand button of the mouse.

Right-click menu ■

When you right-click on a spelling mistake you will see a menu like or similar to this. It is a simpler version of the full spelling window.

Pick options from this menu in the usual way by clicking on them.

> **mistake**
> **misstate**
> **mistaken**
> **mistakes**
>
> Ignore All
> Add
>
> AutoCorrect ▶
> ᴬᴮᶜ✓ Spelling...

Ignore ■

Sometimes the computer picks out a word as a spelling mistake when it isn't a mistake at all. Unusual or modern words, some foreign words and nicknames will not be in the computer's list of words.

The right-click menu and the spelling window both give you an **Ignore All** option. Use this option if the word is not a spelling mistake.

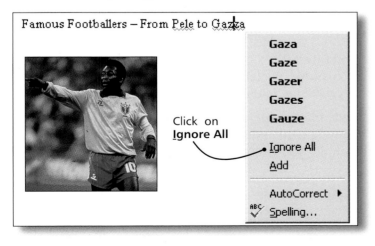

Famous Footballers – From Pele to Gazza

> **Gaza**
> **Gaze**
> **Gazer**
> **Gazes**
> **Gauze**
>
> Ignore All
> Add
>
> AutoCorrect ▶
> ᴬᴮᶜ✓ Spelling...

Click on
Ignore All

Don't ignore! ■

You can make a spelling mistake that the computer will not spot. This happens if you put in the wrong word, for example the words *there* and *their*. If you use the wrong one of these in a sentence the computer won't know that it's a spelling mistake.

Words which are easily confused:

- ● Its and It's
- ● Of and Off
- ● There and Their and They're
- ● Your and You're

The best thing is to learn these common spellings for yourself and get clear about when to use each word.

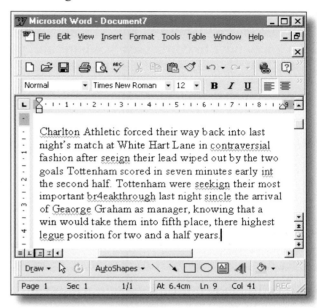

Here is the window of a word processing package. The text that has been entered has a number of spelling mistakes

WHAT YOU HAVE TO DO

Your teacher may have prepared the text file shown above, complete with spelling mistakes. If not, you will need to type it up yourself. Print it out, including all errors.

1. **Correct all the spelling mistakes in the document. Be warned – there is one mistake that the spell check will not find. Can you spot it?**

2. **Print out the corrected version of the file and save it using a new file name.**

Put both versions of the document – with and without errors – into your IT folder.

6. The text files

On the final page in this unit you will learn how to change the way the text is arranged on the page.

Text layout

You already know how to type in a document. You know how to correct the spellings and you know how to change the look of the text.

Now you will learn how to change:

- paragraphs
- tabs
- justification
- margins.

Paragraphs

Remember to break up your text into paragraphs. Make sure you only press the **Enter** key at the end of a paragraph – not at the end of every line.

The break between two paragraphs is sometimes marked by two blank lines. To produce this effect press the **Enter** key twice.

The start of a new paragraph is sometimes marked by an indentation. The first line of the paragraph starts a little way in from the side of the page. To produce this effect, put the cursor at the start of the paragraph and press the **Tab** key.

Tabs

The **Tab** key works by lining up text with invisible **tab stops**. Pressing the **Tab** key is like putting in a group of blank spaces.

You can use the **Tab** key to line up a list of names or numbers to make it easier to read. Below is part of a pupil's timetable:

> **French,** Mr Turnbull, Room Q45, 9.00 – 9.45. **PE,** Ms Patel, Gymn, 9.45 – 10.30. **Maths,** Ms Smith, Room R12, 10.45 – 11.30. **History,** Mr Rose, Room Q15, 11.30 – 12.15

Here is the same information after line breaks and tabs have been added:

French	Mr Turnbull	Room Q45	9.00 – 9.45
PE	Ms Patel	Gymn	9.45 – 10.30
Maths	Ms Smith	Room R12	10.45 – 11.30
History	Mr Rose	Room Q15	11.30 – 12.15

It is now much easier to read.

Tab and paragraph marks

Sometimes word processing packages have been set up to show special text marks where line breaks and tabs have been added.

These marks will not be printed out, they are there to help you while you work on the document. For example, you can delete a tab mark to remove the tab.

Even if these marks are invisible in your word processing package you can still delete them

French→	→	Mr Turnbull	→	Room Q45·	→	9.00	→	·9.45¶
PE →	→	Ms Patel	→	Gymn →	→	9.45	→	·10.30¶
Maths→	→	Ms Smith	→	Room R12	→	10.45	→	·11.30¶
History→	→	Mr Rose	→	Room Q15	→	11.30	→	·12.15¶
¶								

Justification

Text can be **fully justified**, **right** or **left justified**, or **centred**.

Fully justified text has two straight margins, on both the right and left-hand sides. Open a novel or read a newspaper and you will see fully justified text.

Left justified text has a neat left margin, but the text is not lined up on the right-hand side. Many non-fiction books are printed in this style, which is supposed to be easier to read.

Right justified text is pushed over to the right-hand margin. The main place where this type of text is used is at the top of a letter, where you put your address.

Centred text is put in the centre of a line, for example a title or heading.

These buttons on the tool bar allow you to pick what justification you want.

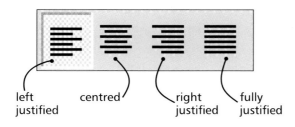

left   centred   right   fully
justified   justified   justified

Pick the justification before you type. Or select a block of text and justify it afterwards.

To remind yourself about how to select a block of text, look back to page 58.

On Target

You should now know how to use a word processor to:

- type documents
- find and correct errors
- change the appearance of the text and layout
- save and print your work.

Margins

The margins of a piece of text are marked on the **ruler** which appears at the top of the working area.

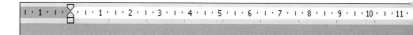

Slide the markers on the ruler to change the indentation and margins.

Books, newspapers, leaflets, etc all use different styles of text and layout

WHAT YOU HAVE TO DO

1. **Type up your school timetable using tabs and line breaks to line it up neatly.**

2. **Take an essay you have already word processed and change it to fully justified. Print out both versions. Which do you like best?**

4 Presentation

On this page you will review the various ways that computers let you present information to an audience.

On Target

In this unit you will learn how to use computers to present information.

- How to combine words and pictures to make posters, handouts and other documents.
- How to record sound clips and store sounds as computer files.
- How to use the computer to store and play video clips.
- How to create presentations and slide shows.

Combining Words and Pictures

You have learned to use computers to make pictures and documents for your school work. In this section you will learn how to put pictures into documents.

Later, when you learn to create other items, such as spreadsheets showing calculations and graphs, you can combine these with pictures and documents using the same techniques.

Words and pictures together are more useful than either on their own. Some information is better expressed in words, and some in pictures. By putting the two together you increase the power of your documents.

Presentations

Sometimes in class you have to give a presentation or talk on a particular subject.

You can give a talk to the class without any aids like charts or handouts.

But sometimes it can be helpful to have visual aids to help with your presentation.

Some information is easier to show in pictures than to describe in words. It is also easier and more fun for the audience to look as well as to listen.

It can be easier for you to have charts and pictures to support your talk. It makes it easier for you to remember what to say next. It gives you a chance to think while people look at the visual material.

Visual Aids

Here are some ways in which you can use visual material in a presentation.

You can pin up a chart or picture. The computer could be used to prepare and print out the posters and sheets you use.

You can write on the blackboard. You don't need the computer for this of course, though you could prepare your notes with a word processor.

You can use an overhead projector. The computer can print out the transparent *acetates* that you use with an overhead projector.

Or you can display visual aids on the screen of your computer while you talk.

This is a good technique for a small presentation, for several reasons:

- the computer screen is bright and colourful
- the presentation can be prepared quickly. You don't have to worry about printing anything out onto paper or acetates
- it is very easy to run through a computer presentation. When you click the mouse button a new picture appears on the computer screen. You don't have to fiddle about with bits of paper or projectors.

But – your whole class might find it difficult to see your computer screen. So this technique is probably better for presenting to a small group. You can get special large screens that you can attach to a computer to let you give a presentation to a big group. Your teacher will tell you if your school has equipment like this.

You will learn how to create computer presentations later in this unit.

Getting IT Right in...

Food Technology

If you were learning about healthy foods you could use the computer to:

- investigate what makes a healthy diet
- present the results in a way that would encourage young people to eat a healthy diet.

Working as a group you could combine pictures and words to make a short leaflet for vegetarians, explaining how to eat a balanced vegetarian diet.

Or you could make a presentation for the rest of the class that displays information about healthy eating on the screen of the computer.

WHAT YOU HAVE TO DO

As a class collect examples of documents which include words and pictures. Bring them to the class.

Pick two examples from these documents. Answer these questions:

1. **What information is shown in words?**

2. **Are the words essential to the document?**

3. **What information is shown in picture form?**

4. **Is the picture essential to the document?**

5. **What impact or impression does the picture give in the document?**

I. Using clip art

On this page you will look at clip art. This is the easiest sort of illustration to use.

Illustrating documents – clip art

Clip art is ready-made electronic art. You can copy it directly into your documents.

Some clip art is provided free with many word processing and graphics packages. You can also buy big sets of clip art on disks or on CD-ROMs. Your school might have a set you can look at to find pictures to put into your work.

Clip art collections usually consist of black and white and coloured drawings. Sometimes they include photographs, sounds and videos too.

The advantage of clip art is that it is made by professional artists so it is of high quality. The disadvantage is that you might not be able to find clip art on the exact subject you need. Some images in this book are clip art.

Inserting clip art

The simplest way to add clip art to a document is to use the clip art that is provided with the word processing package. This is what you do:

● Use the **Insert** menu to place an item into a word processed document

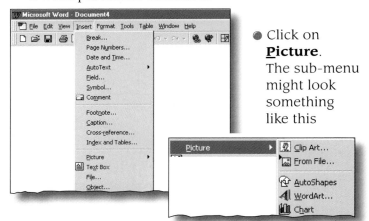

● Click on **Picture**. The sub-menu might look something like this

● Select **Clip Art...**

The clip art window of a typical word processing package will look something like the window on the left.

You can search for what you want under different categories.

● Click on the image you want to select. It will be placed into your document

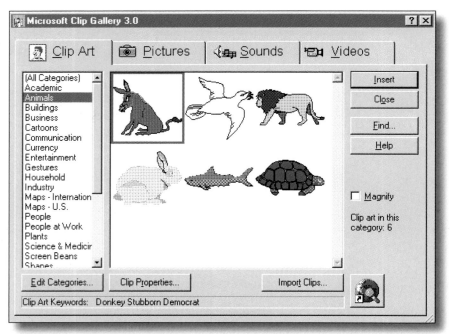

Safety in the computer room *p14*   Creating original graphics *p32*

Move and resize ■

Once a picture has been placed in a document you can:

● change its size, and

● move it to a new location.

You nearly always have to do these things. You have to make sure the picture fits in properly with the rest of your work.

The way you move and resize pictures will vary between different word processing packages. On the right is just one example.

Copyright

The artists who work to produce clip art need to be paid for what they do. When somebody produces an item which is easy to copy (like a song or a picture) they are protected by the law of **copyright**.

This means that you only have the right to copy the material if you have proper permission.

Some clip art is completely free to use. Some you have to pay for in full. You may be allowed to use the clip art as often as you like once you have paid for it.

In other cases, for example with high quality photos, you might only have the right to use it once per payment.

It can also make a difference if you intend to sell your work (in a book or magazine, for example), or if it will be given away free (such as in a sales brochure).

In other words – copyright is complicated. You need to check before you use other people's artwork or photographs. Your teacher will let you know about your rights to use any of the material available on the school system.

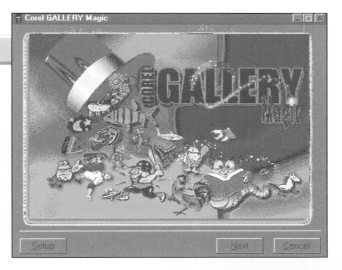

Corel *GALLERY Magic* is an example of a commercial product offering 200,000 clip art images on a set of CDs

WHAT YOU HAVE TO DO

1. Look at page 14 to remind yourself about working safely in the computer room. Pick one piece of advice about health and safety.

2. Use a word processing package or a graphics package to design a poster to present the piece of advice you have chosen. Use a font style and size that is clear and easy to read.

3. Find a suitable item of clip art to go with your message. Place, move and resize it in your document.

Save the file. Print it out. Keep the print-out in your IT folder.

2. Swap shop

Next you will learn some of the skills you need in order to place an image you have created into a text document.

Opening packages and copying pictures

It is useful to be able to illustrate documents with clip art. But it is even more useful to be able to copy your own pictures and graphs into documents.

One big advantage of Windows software is that you can open more than one software package at the same time. In this way you can have both your picture and your document open at the same time. You can also swap between them. This is the first step you need to take if you want to put the picture into the document.

Opening several packages

To remind yourself about how to start up a software package turn to page 24.

If you have opened one software package the window might fill the entire screen. It is still possible to start up another package.

● Use the **Start** button to start another package. Look for the task bar and Start button at the bottom of the screen

Another method is to shrink the open window to a button on the task bar. You will then be able to see the rest of the desktop and look for the icons you need.

Swapping between packages

Once you have started up two or more packages it is easy to swap between them while you work. If the windows are half-screen size you can see both of them on the screen at the same time.

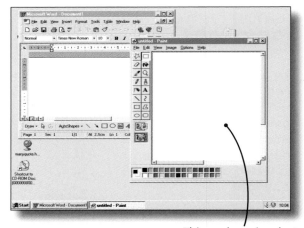

This package is selected

● Click on the window of the package you want to use next. It will move to the front and you can work with it

Now this package is selected

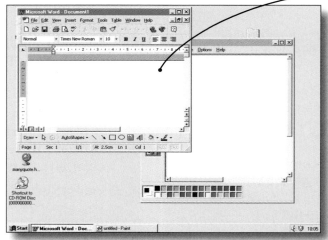

If the windows are full screen size then you can't use this method of swapping between windows.

Instead you can use the buttons on the task bar. There is a button for each software package that is open.

● Click on the button of the package you want to use

Loading software *p24*

Open both files

If you want to put a picture into a document you have to:

- open the picture file
- open the document file.

For example, a pupil was learning about levers.

Here is what she wrote about levers.

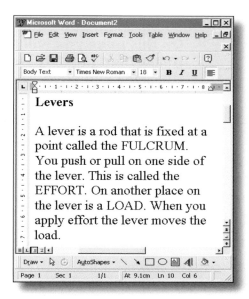

She thought her words would be easier to understand if she drew a picture. This is the picture she drew, using computer graphics.

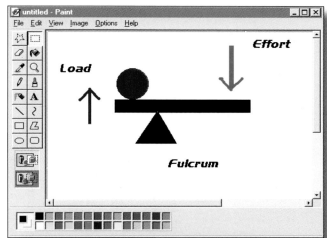

She opened both of these files at once.

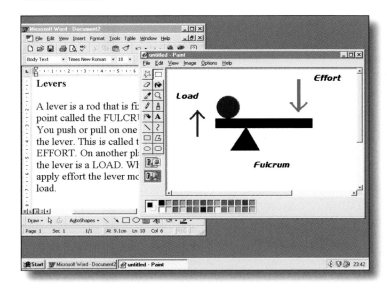

On the next page you will see how the pupil copied the picture into the document.

WHAT YOU HAVE TO DO

In the exercise on the last page you discussed health and safety with your teacher and the rest of the class.

Open a graphics package you have used before. Use the graphics package to create a picture illustrating a point about health and safety. Here is a simple example. It illustrates the point *don't take drinks into the computer room.* Copy this example or develop an image of your own choice.

Save and print out the picture and put it into your IT folder.

3. All together now

On this page you will learn how to select a picture, copy it and then paste it into a text document. These are all the skills you need to illustrate documents with your own pictures.

Putting a picture into a document

You know how to make pictures using a **Graphics** package.

You know how to make documents using a **Word Processing** package.

By putting pictures into documents you make them both more useful.

On this page you will learn how to make use of the skills you have learned. You will learn how to select a picture, copy it and then paste it into a text document.

Prepare both files

Before you start to copy a picture into a document:

● Open the picture file using a graphics package
● Open the document file using a word processing package

To remind yourself how to open both files at once look on the previous page.

Selecting items

Before you copy an item you have to select it.

There are two main ways in which an item can be selected:

● Drag the mouse pointer across the item – this will work with Bitmap graphics, for example
● Click on the item to select it – this will work with Vector graphics, for example, or clip art

Select all

If you want to select all your work, for example a complete picture, then use **Select All**, which is an option in the **Edit** menu.

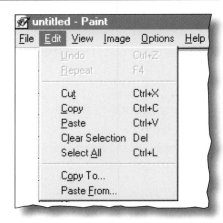

Cut, copy and paste

Here is a reminder about cut, copy and paste.

● Cut – the selected item is deleted and placed in computer memory.
● Copy – the item is placed in computer memory without deleting it.
● Paste – the item in computer memory is inserted into the file.

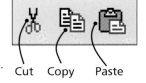

Cut   Copy   Paste

Swap package ■

● Swap over to the word processing package. Use the task bar at the bottom of the screen. Click on the button with the name of the word processing package

Move and paste ■

Where do you want the picture to be in the document? At the top? Halfway through?

Move the cursor to the place where you want the picture to appear. Remember:

● the cursor is the flashing line which shows where your words will appear when you type
● you move the cursor with the arrow keys, or by clicking with the mouse pointer.

If you need to remind yourself about moving the cursor look on page 52.

When the cursor is in the right position, **paste** the picture into the document. The easiest way is to click on the **Paste** icon.

Resize the picture ■

The picture you have inserted should be surrounded by a border, or by resize handles. If it isn't marked in this way then try clicking on it with the mouse pointer.

Drag the resize handles to change the size and shape of the picture

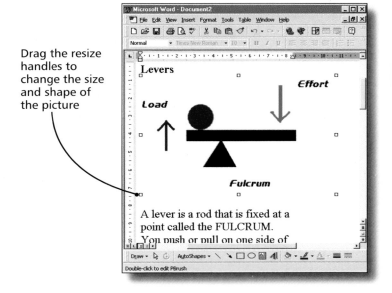

Move the picture ■

The chances are that the picture isn't in exactly the right place. It is easy to move the picture, generally by **dragging** it using the mouse.

If the picture isn't marked with handles or a border then select it, by clicking on it, before you try to move it.

Your work should now be complete.

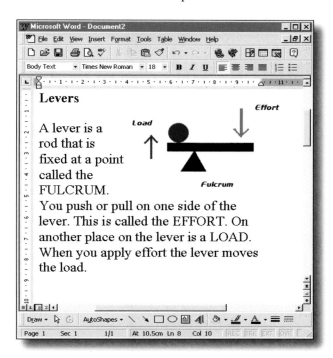

This example uses a graphics package. However, you can also select and insert other items from the packages you will learn about later in this book.

WHAT YOU HAVE TO DO

In the exercise on the last page you created an illustration and a handout about health and safety.

Using the techniques shown on this page copy the picture into the handout document. Move and resize the picture to position it in just the right place in the handout – next to the point it illustrates.

Save and print the illustrated handout and keep it in your IT folder.

4. Many media

Multimedia means work on a computer that includes words, pictures, sounds and moving images.

On this page you will look at the type of multimedia tools that are available on modern computers.

Multimedia materials

So far in this book you have looked at presenting data on paper. You have looked at creating essays, reports, posters and other paper-based documents.

Paper materials are very important. They will continue to be used for many years to come. However the use of computers opens up a whole new area of presentations: using computers themselves to present information.

What does this mean? Instead of people looking at your work on paper, they look at it on the screen of the computer. And the big difference is that you can include new types of material, not just words and pictures. You can also include moving images and sounds to help get your message across.

Playing audio

Multimedia presentations can include sounds.

Sounds can be stored in computer files. Many sound files end with the three letters **WAV**. The icon of a sound file will tell you that the file holds sound or music. Here are two examples.

If you double-click on the icon it will play the sound. The display on the screen will look something like this.

There is more than one type of software available. The computer will pick the right kind for the selected file.

Playing video

There are also files which store moving images, for example film clips. Once again the file icon shows you that the file contains film. One common type of video clip ends with the three letters **AVI**.

To look at video clips you need to have special software. The software to look at an AVI file is provided free with *Windows 95* and *Windows 98*. So to look at this type of clip you simply double-click on a file icon that ends .**avi**.

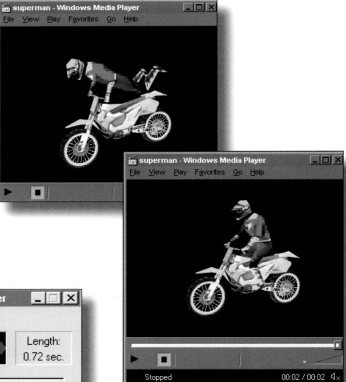

Copyright *p67* Search the Internet *p102* Obtain items from the Internet *p114*

Recording your own sound clips ■

The same application that plays WAV files will allow you to record your own sound files. Your computer must be fitted with a microphone.

To start the application, open the **Programs** menu and the **Accessories** folder from the **Start** button. Look for the **Multimedia** folder. In here is a range of software packages related to multimedia.

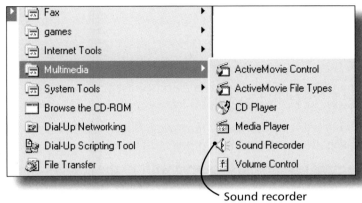

Sound recorder

The application *Sound Recorder* will let you record sound through the microphone of your computer. It will store it as a **.wav** file. It could be your own voice, a piece of music, or a sound effect, for example.

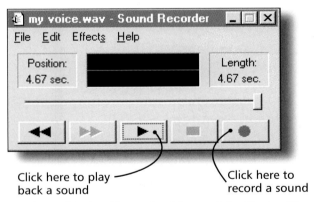

Click here to play back a sound

Click here to record a sound

You can also edit the file and add special effects, like speeding it up, or adding echo.

Here is the icon for the resulting audio file. Double-click on this file to play the recorded sound.

my voice.wav

Recording video ■

Recording video is much more difficult than audio. You need special software and hardware, which is not provided free with a typical computer.

Multimedia clips ■

As well as recording your own sound and video clips you can obtain a wide range of multimedia clips from CD-ROMs and the Internet. Many of these can be copied onto your computer for your private use. However, remember that copyright rules apply to multimedia materials.

Warning!

A typical AVI (video) file is very large in size. It will take a long time to copy onto your computer, and it will take up a lot of computer memory.

WHAT YOU HAVE TO DO

1. **Look for audio and video clips which are available:**

    ■ **on your computer**

    ■ **over the school network**

    ■ **on CD-ROMs.**

    Play any clips which you find. Copy one or two onto your storage area.

2. **If your computer has a microphone, record your own sound clip and save it in your storage area. See if you can record the following clips:**

    ■ **the sound of applause**

    ■ **the sound of a book closing**

    ■ **the sound of a laugh.**

3. **Use a word processing package to create a document with full details of what multimedia clips you have found, and what clips you have created.**

5. Getting it together (I)

Over the next few pages you will learn to use Microsoft *PowerPoint*. This package lets you create a multimedia computer presentation using words and pictures.

Putting together *PowerPoint* presentations

It is not difficult to create on-screen presentations which include all the types of multimedia materials. Someone looking through the on-screen presentation will be able to read text, listen to sounds, and look at both pictures and moving images.

Creating complex multimedia presentations is an advanced topic. It is covered more fully in the next book in this series.

Microsoft *PowerPoint* is a special package designed to make it easy for you to put together a multimedia presentation. It quickly creates a series of **slides**. Each slide can contain words and pictures.

When you have prepared the presentation, *PowerPoint* makes it easy for you to run through the slides on the screen of your computer.

You may have a slightly different presentation package in your school. Your teacher will be able to tell you what the differences are.

Start up

PowerPoint can be started from the **Start** menu, or by clicking on an icon.

Microsoft PowerPoint

PowerPoint offers many features which make it easy to create a presentation.

Templates have been set up with all the colours and text options organised for you. This is very useful.

AutoContent wizard will create a complete structured presentation on a typical business subject (like a financial report). This is useful for business people.

When you start up, a screen lets you choose between these options. You can also open a blank screen or a presentation you made earlier.

● Click on **Template**
● Click **OK**

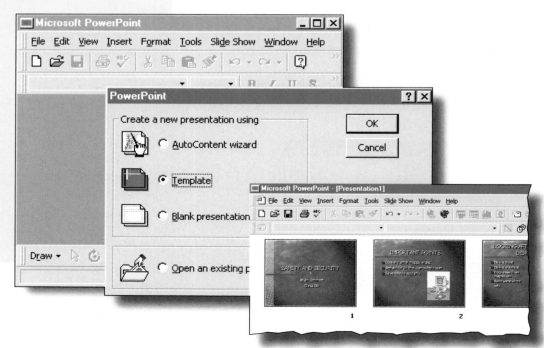

Templates

More than a dozen presentation templates have been designed for you.

- Click on each template and check out what it looks like

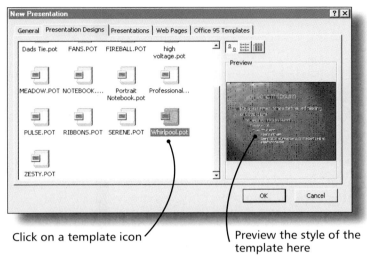

Click on a template icon

Preview the style of the template here

- Each template uses different colours and designs. When you have found the one you like best click on the **OK** button to pick that template

Pick a slide design

Now you are ready to design the first slide of your presentation. Will it be words only? Words and pictures?

The next screen you see offers you a range of typical slide designs.

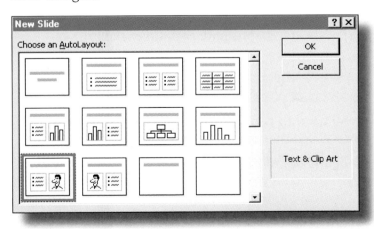

Pick the type of slide you want to make first. You can make the slides in any order and reorganise them later (see page 78 for more information about reorganising slides).

Slide outline

In this example you can see how to make a slide from the middle of the presentation, which includes words and pictures.

Here is the outline of a slide, ready for you to add words and pictures.

- Click in the text boxes. Type the words you want to add to the slide

Adding pictures

If you double-click on the picture box you will see the clip art window. This is very similar to the clip art window used in Microsoft *Word*. To remind yourself about this look back to page 66.

Click here to insert

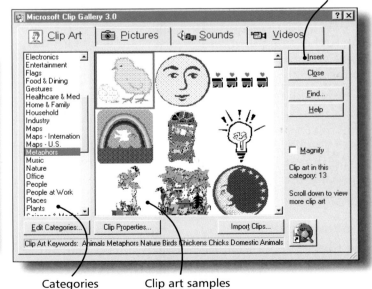

Categories   Clip art samples

- Select a category, and a piece of clip art
- Click on the **Insert** button to put it into your slide

6. Getting it together (2)

The next stage is to add your own materials. This might be text, pictures, sounds or video.

Add your own materials ■

Here is a slide that is nearly completed. A picture has been added, and most of the words.

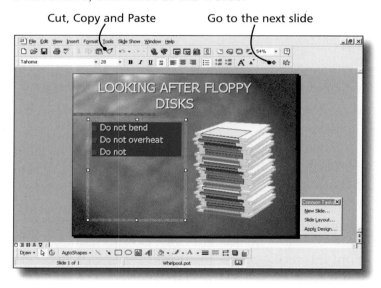

Cut, Copy and Paste   Go to the next slide

The tool bar of *PowerPoint* includes the icons for **cut, copy** and **paste**. You can copy and paste your own materials into a *PowerPoint* presentation from other software packages.

New slide

Once you have finished the slide click on **New Slide** in the **Insert** menu to make the next slide of the presentation. Keep adding slides until the presentation is complete.

Look and edit

Use the scroll bar to move between slides. You can edit (make changes to) the slides at any time.

Save

You can save the presentation in the normal way, from the **File** menu.

Adding video and audio ■

Next you will learn how to make your presentations even more interesting by adding **sounds** and **moving images**.

Some clips of sound and images are included with *PowerPoint*. You will also see how you can include clips which you have found for yourself, for example on a CD-ROM.

Add extra items ■

You can add extra items to your *PowerPoint* presentation at any time, using the tool bar.

Word
processed
document

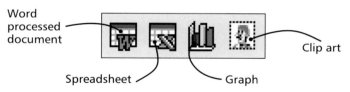

Clip art

Spreadsheet   Graph

You can add word processed documents, spreadsheets, graphs and, of course, clip art.

Adding sound ■

If you want to add sound pick the tool for **clip art**. You will see the clip art window.

Along the top of the clip art window there are some *tabs*. These let you pick different types of items to add to the presentation.

You can add:

- normal clip art
- sound clips
- photographs
- video clips.

● Click on the **Sounds** tab. You will see this selection:

Tabs — Play sound — Insert sound into presentation

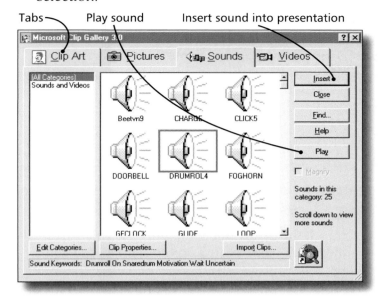

The sound clips have descriptive names. You can listen to a clip by selecting it and clicking on the **Play** button.

● When you have chosen the clip you want, click on the **Insert** button to put it into your presentation

This is what a presentation screen looks like with a sound clip added to it.

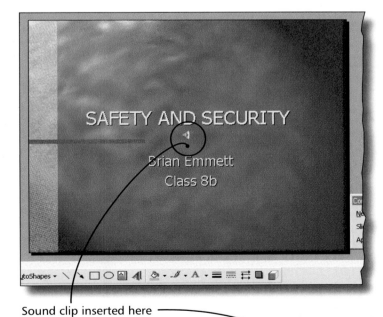

Sound clip inserted here —

The place where the sound clip has been added is marked with a symbol. During the presentation you can click on this symbol with the mouse pointer and the sound will play.

Adding video

● Click on the final tab in the clip art window. You will see a selection of video clips
● Use the **Play** button to run a clip. Use the **Insert** button to add a clip to a presentation slide

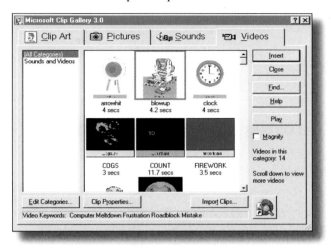

The selected clip shows a computer blowing up. Quite a good clip for a presentation on computer safety!

When the clip is added to the presentation the first frame of the clip is shown on the screen. When you are giving the presentation you can click on this image with the mouse pointer and it will run through its movement.

If you have sound and video clips from elsewhere which you would like to add to the presentation, you can insert them into any slide.

● Open the **Insert** menu. Pick **Movies and Sounds**

The small menu that appears gives you several options including:

● add a movie from a file
● add a sound from a file
● record a new sound.

WHAT YOU HAVE TO DO

Create a presentation of at least five *PowerPoint* slides on *Safety in the Computer Room*. Your presentation must include pictures as well as words on at least some slides.

Make sure you save your presentation.

7. Power presentation

On the last page in this unit you will see how to give a presentation using the *PowerPoint* slides you have made.

Giving the presentation

You have planned a *PowerPoint* presentation that includes words, pictures and sound or video.

This work is now all ready for you to give a live presentation to the class. Here you will see how to give a *PowerPoint* presentation.

Review your presentation

First you need to look through your presentation.

There are a number of different ways to *view* the presentation.

● Open the **View** menu

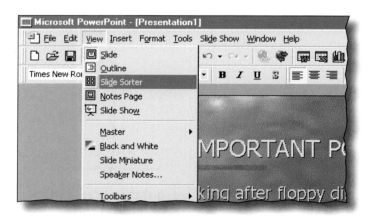

● Pick from one of these options:
- **Slide** – view and edit one slide at a time. This is the view you have used up to now
- **Outline** – just shows the words from the presentation
- **Slide Sorter** – shows all the slides at once
- **Slide Show** – lets you give the presentation

Slide sorter

If you pick the **Slide Sorter** option you will see all the slides you have created on the screen. You can quickly check through your presentation. If you want to, you can drag the slides to new positions and reorganise the order in which they appear.

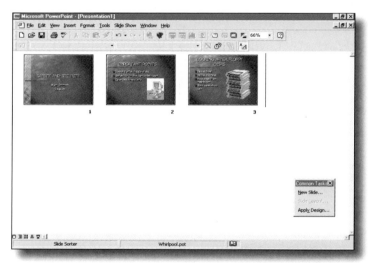

Presenting from the computer

In general the best way to give a *PowerPoint* presentation is from the computer. The slides you designed are displayed on the screen – everyone can look at them. Meanwhile you can do the talking that goes with the slides.

Make sure everyone in the audience can see the computer screen. If you are going to use audio, make sure the volume control on your computer is turned up. Hold the mouse ready.

Use the **View** menu to pick **Slide Show**. The presentation begins.

Begin your presentation

When you begin your presentation the *PowerPoint* tool bar and all the other software features will disappear. All that will be seen on the screen is your first slide, filling the whole screen.

If there are audio or video clips on the slide, click on them with the mouse pointer when you are ready to run the clips.

When you are ready to go on to the next slide, click anywhere with the mouse pointer.

If you want to stop the presentation in the middle, click the **Escape** button on the keyboard.

Otherwise, when you click on the final slide, the presentation will finish and the software window will come back on the screen.

On Target

You should now know how to use computers to present information.

■ How to combine words and pictures to make posters, handouts and other documents.

■ How to record sound clips and store sounds as computer files.

■ How to use the computer to store and play video clips.

■ How to create presentations and slide shows.

WHAT YOU HAVE TO DO

1. **Run through your presentation carefully. Check everything is working correctly. Make sure you know what you are going to say with each slide.**

2. **Give your presentation to the rest of your class, or to a small group.**

3. **Afterwards, evaluate how it went.**

   ■ **Did it run smoothly?**
   ■ **Did your audience understand the main points you were making?**

INTRODUCTION

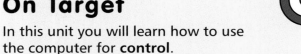

5 In Control

Can you write a series of instructions that will tell the computer what to do? This unit will show you how.

On Target

In this unit you will learn how to use the computer for **control**.

You will discover how to type in a sequence of commands that control a small robot, called a *turtle*. This involves being able to:

- type in computer commands
- spot and correct errors
- pick the right commands in the right order.

You may have a real turtle robot at school. If not you will have a program that will simulate the movement of the robot on screen.

Recording a Sequence of Instructions

In this book you have learned many different ways to control the computer. For example you can give instructions to the computer by picking a choice from a menu, or by clicking on an icon.

Now you are going to learn about another way of controlling the computer: by storing a series of instructions. Instead of giving instructions one at a time to the computer, you store them in a file. Then when you **run** the file the computer will carry out all the stored instructions.

You can sit back and the computer will carry out one instruction after another, without you doing anything.

You have to make sure that you have given the right instructions, in the right order.

Programming

Have you heard of computer **programming**? The job of a computer programmer is to write instructions for the computer. The instructions tell the computer what to do. A computer program is a series of stored instructions.

Robotics and Control

One use of a series of stored instructions is so that the computer can **control** machines.

Machines that are attached to computers can work on their own, without a person in control. For example, a machine in a car park will:

- read your ticket
- tell you how much to pay
- count the money you pay
- open the barrier to let you out.

All of these actions are controlled by a computer.

 Software *p12*   Starting Logo *p82*

A robot is a machine that has a computer inside it. The computer enables the robot to move around doing different jobs. Robots don't really look like people. They are designed to do particular jobs and their shape suits the job they have to do.

Hank Morgan

This robot can pick up objects

Logo

Logo is a system which lets you store a series of instructions. It is a programming **language**. It is designed for use in schools. **Mach Turtles *Logo*** is the example used in this book.

You can do many things with Logo. The original use of Logo in schools was to control a small robot. The robot is called the *turtle*. Actually it isn't a real robot because it doesn't have a computer inside it. It is controlled by your computer.

You can give instructions like

forward 10, right

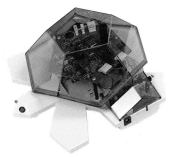

The turtle will roll forward a short way, then turn to the right.

Simulation

Of course it is good fun to control a real device that rolls around on the floor. But it can be a bit difficult to organise. How could everyone in the class get a chance to use the turtle?

Instead many Logo packages show you a turtle on the computer screen. You can give instructions and see the turtle move.

This might be how your computer system works at school.

Mach Turtles Logo
Learning Edition

Version 1.00
This version expires June 30, 1999

Copyright © 1996-1998 Mach Turtles Software Inc. All rights reserved.

Drawing with a Pen

When people use Logo to control the robot turtle they usually spread paper on the floor. The robot turtle holds a pen. As it rolls around on the floor it leaves a line everywhere it goes.

This is very useful. By looking at the line you can check up on what the turtle did. You can see where it rolled.

The same thing happens when you use the turtle on the screen. As it moves about the screen it leaves a line. As you learn to use Logo you will learn to make the turtle draw different shapes on the screen.

The Logo turtle marks its trail on the screen

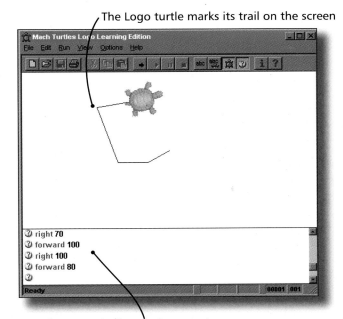

These are the instructions used

WHAT YOU HAVE TO DO

Investigate the version of Logo which is available at your school.

1. What is the name of this version of Logo?

2. Is there a turtle robot available that you can connect to a computer?

3. Does the package display a turtle on the screen that you can control?

Put the answers to these questions into your IT folder.

Make sure you know how to start up and close down the Logo package.

I. At the interface

First of all you will look at the interface used with Logo and learn to give a simple command to control the turtle.

Starting to use Logo

The **Logo** interface will let you:

- give instructions to the turtle
- see how the turtle moves on the screen
- read messages from the computer
- give other instructions to the computer (like **Save**).

Many different companies have made versions of Logo. Each version will have a slightly different interface. The version you use at school might have a different interface from the version used in this book.

But this doesn't matter – it's still Logo. Even if your version of Logo looks different, it will still understand the same commands.

The interface

Below is an example of a Logo interface. This is what it looks like when you start up Logo, before you give any commands.

The interface has two **windows**. In one window you can see the words you type. In the big window at the top of the screen you can see the turtle and the trail it leaves as it moves.

Your Logo might not have exactly this interface but it will have a system that lets you give commands and see the turtle move. In any case it will use the same Logo commands described here.

Giving commands

It is easy to give commands to the turtle. You just type them in. The commands you type can be seen on the screen. The pupil using Logo has typed in the command **forward 150**.

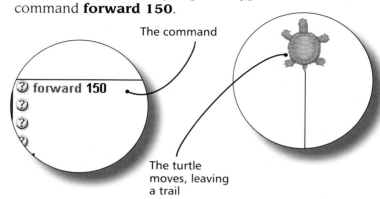

The command

> forward 150

The turtle moves, leaving a trail

A question mark is displayed in the window. The command appears after the question mark.

When you press the **Enter** key the computer carries out the command. A new question mark appears. You can type a new command when you are ready.

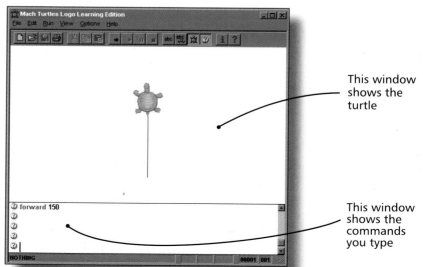

This window shows the turtle

This window shows the commands you type

i Logo commands in full *p87*

One small step

One thing you might notice from the picture is that turtle steps are tiny. Going forward 150 steps doesn't take the turtle too far up the screen.

This is very convenient for you. It means you can give very precise instructions to the turtle. By changing the number (to 149, say, or to 151) you can precisely control where the turtle is on the screen. For now the examples will use *round* numbers like 150 and 160.

Errors

It is very easy to mistype one of the instructions. A pupil typed **forawrd** instead of **forward**.

The computer displays a **message** to tell you that it doesn't understand. The turtle has not moved. If this happens don't worry, just retype the instruction more carefully and the computer will understand it.

Stop work

When you have looked at the interface and given a command then you might wish to stop work.

The version of Logo shown on this page has a menu system. You click on a menu name to open it, and click on an option in the menu to select it.

Open the first menu. **Exit** is the final option on this menu. Your version of Logo might have a different way to exit. If so, your teacher will tell you.

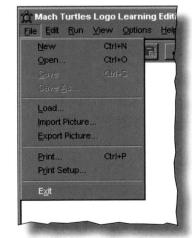

IT at work

The job of a computer programmer is to write instructions to control the computer. This includes instructions that control the display on the computer screen. Often these displays are very detailed and complex.

```
void CCircCtrl::FlashColor(CDC* pdc)
{
        CBrush* pOldBrush;
        CBrush flashBrush(TranslateColor(m_flashColor));
        CPen* pOldPen;
        Crect rc;

        GetClientRect(rc);
        GetDrawRect(&rc);
        pOldBrush = pdc->SelectObject(&flashBrush);
        pOldPen = (Cpen*)pdc->SelectStockObject(BLACK_PEN);
        pdc->Ellipse(rc);
        pdc->SelectObject(pOldPen);
        pdc->SelectObject(pOldBrush);
}
```

Programmers who create the latest computer games need to work out the instructions for the graphics you see. This is made even more complex when things change in 3D as you play the game.

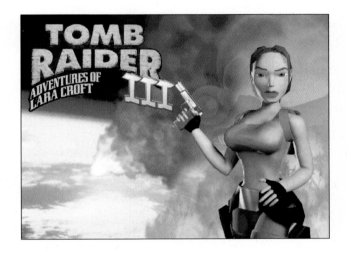

WHAT YOU HAVE TO DO

Start up Logo. Look at the interface. See if you can find the areas described on this page:

1. Type in the command **FORWARD 30**. Observe how the turtle moves.

2. Type in the command **FORAWRD 30**. Observe the error message.

3. Exit from Logo.

2. Turning turtle

Here you will learn how to give more commands to the Logo turtle, making it turn and move in different directions.

Moving the turtle

So far you have used one command – **forward**. This command makes the turtle move forward, leaving a trail behind it. On this page you will learn the commands to make the turtle turn to the right or left, so that it can move off in a new direction.

Turning left

To make the turtle turn to the left you type the command **left** followed by a number.

Below, a pupil has typed the command **left 90**.

A matter of degree

The number after the instruction tells the turtle how many **degrees** to turn.

You probably know how to measure angles using degrees.

180 degrees turns the turtle round so that it faces back the way it came.

360 degrees turns the turtle completely round so that it is back where it started.

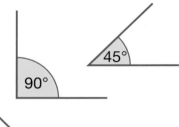

The turtle is now facing to the left

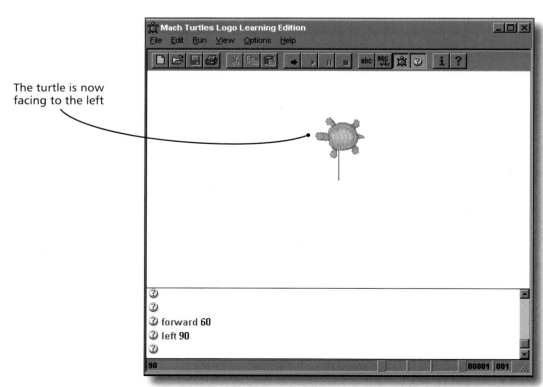

New directions

After turning you can make the turtle go forward again in the new direction. In the example below the pupil has typed **forward 60**. The turtle has moved forward 60 in the new direction it is facing.

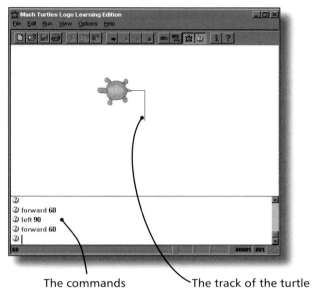

The commands   The track of the turtle

Notice that when you tell the turtle to go forward it goes forward in whatever direction it is pointing. It won't go up the screen unless it is pointing in that direction to start with.

Turning right

To make the turtle turn to the right you give the command **right** followed by a number.

In this example a pupil gave the commands:

forward 50   **right 90**   **forward 100**

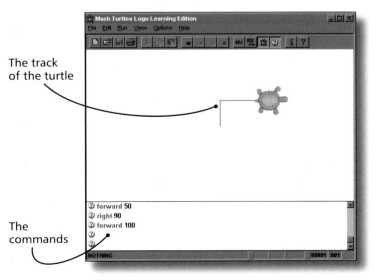

The track of the turtle

The commands

Left and right

Remember when you tell the turtle to turn **right** or **left** it turns to *its* right or left. So you have to pay attention to which way the turtle is facing when you give the command.

In this example the turtle is facing to the right. The pupil gives the commands:

> **right 90**
>
> **forward 50**

The turtle turns 90 degrees to its right. This means it is facing down the screen. When it moves it draws a line going down the screen.

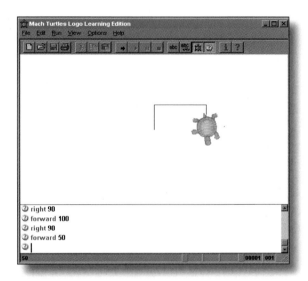

WHAT YOU HAVE TO DO

1. **Start up Logo and enter the five commands shown here:**

   FORWARD 50

   RIGHT 90

   FORWARD 100

   RIGHT 90

   FORWARD 50

2. **Type in two more commands which will return the turtle to the starting position, with its track marking out a rectangle on the screen.**

3. In command

On this page you will review all the commands which you need to use to make the turtle draw shapes on the screen, and learn how to print out the results.

Draw and print

On this page you will learn two new Logo commands – commands which let you clear the screen, and move the turtle backwards.

You will also review all the commands that you have learned so far.

You will learn how commands can be abbreviated to make them easier to type.

Finally, you will learn how to print out the contents of the different windows, so that you have a printed record of your work.

Clear screen ▪

As you give commands to the turtle it draws a line on the screen. After a while the screen might get a bit cluttered.

The command **Clearscreen** lets you start afresh.

When you type **Clearscreen** (all one word) the turtle returns to its starting position at the centre of the screen. All the lines it has drawn are cleared away.

Getting IT Right in...

Mathematics

If you are learning about geometry you could use the Logo programming language to investigate different geometric shapes. By typing commands you could make the turtle draw different shapes.

Back ▪

You have learned to use the command **Forward** to make the turtle move forward. To make the computer move backwards you give the command **Back** followed by a number. The number stands for the number of turtle steps.

In the example below, a pupil cleared the screen and then made the turtle move back by 75 steps.

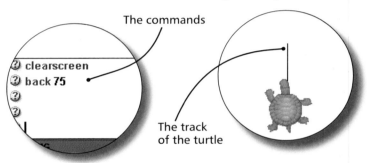

The commands

② clearscreen
② back 75
②
②

The track of the turtle

Command review ▪

Here are the main commands that let you move the turtle. **n** stands for any number.

● In these commands the number tells the turtle how many steps to walk.

    FORWARD *n*

    BACK *n*

● In these commands the number tells the turtle how many degrees to turn.

    RIGHT *n*

    LEFT *n*

● This command clears the screen and returns the turtle to its starting position.

    CLEARSCREEN

Rules of command

There are only a few rules about how you type commands.

It doesn't matter whether you type the commands in capital letters, lower case letters, or a mixture of the two. For example:

Left 90

LEFT 90

left 90

You must always leave at least one space between the command and the number.

Left 90	This command is OK
Left 90	This command is OK
Left90	This command is not OK

Here is a list of commands entered by a pupil. Can you spot which commands have got errors in them?

? CLEarscreeN

? BACK

? Left   45

? forward80

? FORWARD 100

Abbreviations

You have learned five commands. Each of these commands can be replaced with a two-letter abbreviation.

BACK	**= BK**
CLEARSCREEN	**= CS**
FORWARD	**= FD**
LEFT	**= LT**
RIGHT	**= RT**

Instead of typing the whole command you can use the abbreviation instead.

CLEARSCREEN	**= CS**
FORWARD 80	**= FD 80**
RIGHT 90	**= RT 90**
BACK 60	**= BK 60**

Print

The Logo interface lets you print out the commands you have given, and the results of these commands.

If you are using **Mach Turtles *Logo*** select **Print** from the **File** menu and you will see this window.

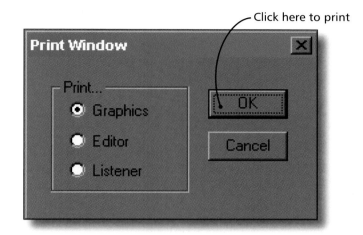

Click here to print

- Pick Graphics to print out the track the turtle has marked on the screen
- Pick Listener to print out a list of all the commands you have given so far

Your teacher will tell you if your version of Logo has a different command.

WHAT YOU HAVE TO DO

Start up the version of Logo that you are going to use.

Make sure you understand how to give commands to the turtle, and how you can see the turtle's movements.

1. **Enter the commands that make the turtle draw a square on the screen, each side 50 steps long.**

Make sure you know how to print from the Logo interface.

2. **Print out your commands and the square the turtle drew.**

3. **Use Clearscreen to erase the square you drew, ready for a new exercise.**

Keep your work in your IT folder.

4. Now in colour

The next step is to use different colours and styles of pen to make your Logo work more interesting and attractive.

Adding some colour

As the turtle runs along on the floor – or on the screen – it draws with a pen. By looking at the line the turtle leaves you can see the effect of your instructions.

But the turtle can do more than this. You have a choice of pens for example. You can change the width and colour of the pen. By changing the pen you can change the type of line that the turtle draws.

Choosing the colour

The colour choices in Mach Turtles *Logo* are shown by a colon (:) followed by the name of a colour. You can select from these colour names:

:Red	**:Green**	**:Cyan** (this means light turquoise)
:Blue	**:Yellow**	**:Brown**
:Magenta	**:Gray**	**:Black**
:White		

There are also darker versions of some of these colours:

:Darkred	**:Darkgreen**	**:Darkcyan**
:Darkblue	**:Darkpink**	**:Darkgray**

Some of the colours available with Logo

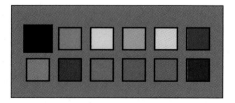

NB Because Mach Turtles *Logo* is a Canadian package it uses the American/Canadian spellings (for example Gray instead of Grey and Color instead of Colour)

Set pen colour

To change the colour of the line the turtle draws, use this command:

> **SetPenColor** (all one word)

So to change the line to **red** enter the command:

> **Setpencolor :red**

To change the line to **blue** enter the command:

> **Setpencolor :blue**

Luckily there is an abbreviation for **setpencolor**. Simply type **SetPC**.

> **Set PC :red**
>
> **SetPC :blue**

Drawing in colour

By varying the colours used in drawings you can produce some attractive effects.

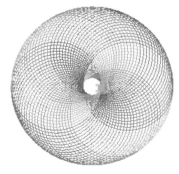

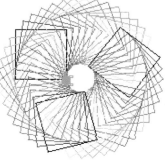

While you are learning to use Logo it's better to stick to one colour at a time

Use of colour p42

Pen up, pen down

Sometimes you want the turtle to move without leaving a line. You can make the turtle lift its pen up so that it doesn't leave a line. The command for this is:

PenUP

This can be abbreviated to:

PU

After you have given this command you can move the turtle about as usual. Commands like **forward** and **back** will still work. But the turtle will not leave a line as it moves. You can move the turtle to a new position without making a line.

When you have moved the turtle to a new part of the screen you might want to start drawing again. You want to make the turtle draw with the pen. The command to bring the pen down again, so that the turtle draws, is:

PenDOWN

This can be abbreviated to:

PD

For example:

A pupil programmed the turtle to walk across the screen, drawing different coloured squares.

The squares the pupil drew

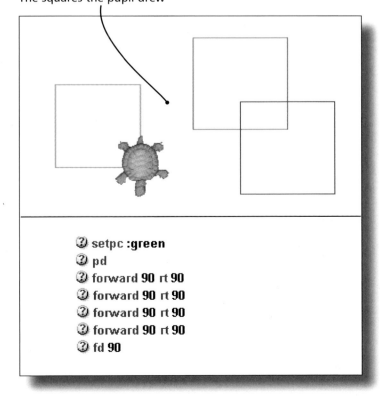

```
② setpc :green
② pd
② forward 90 rt 90
② forward 90 rt 90
② forward 90 rt 90
② forward 90 rt 90
② fd 90
```

In the window at the bottom of the last column you can see some of the commands that the pupil gave. He used **PD** (Pen Down) as well as **SetPC** (Set Pen Colour). He also used the drawing commands you have learned on earlier pages, such as **RT** (Right) and **FD** (Forward).

- Do you understand the meaning of each of these commands?
- Which part of the picture is drawn by these commands?

Pen width

You can change the width of the pen that the turtle holds. There are five pen widths. They are numbered 1 to 5.

To pick a pen width, type **SetPenWidth** (all one word) and the number of the width you want. For example:

SetPenWidth 5

SetPenWidth is abbreviated to **SetPW**, so you would also give the command:

SetPW 5

For example, a pupil used Logo to draw this rainbow.

WHAT YOU HAVE TO DO

1. Draw a line 120 steps long. Then change the colour. Continue to draw the line for another 120 steps. Keep changing the colour every 120 steps.

2. Draw the rainbow of lines shown on this page. Use a wide pen.

3. Draw three shapes on the screen. Use three different colours. Use **pen up** and **pen down** to make sure that the turtle does not draw a line between the shapes.

Print out your results and the commands that you used. Put the print-out into your IT folder.

5. Getting into shape

On the final page of this unit you will look at ways of using the Logo commands that you have learned. You will see how you can use Logo to make the turtle draw different geometrical shapes.

Making shapes

You have learned to use many different commands to control the Logo turtle. Here are the commands you have learned. If you don't remember how to use any of these commands, look back over the previous few pages.

In these commands the letter *n* stands for any number.

Command	Abbreviation
CLEARSCREEN	CS
FORWARD *n*	FD *n*
BACK *n*	BK *n*
LEFT *n*	LT *n*
RIGHT *n*	RT *n*
PENUP	PU
PENDOWN	PD
SETPENCOLOR :[red]	SETPC :[red]
SETPENWIDTH *n*	SETPW *n*

By putting these commands together you can make the computer draw different shapes on the screen.

On this page you will look at several different shapes and the commands you need to give to draw those shapes.

All square

One of the easiest shapes to draw is a square.

The only decision you have to make is how big you want the square to be. This is the number of steps you tell the turtle to move.

If you want a big square tell the turtle to move a lot of steps, perhaps 80. If you want a little square tell the turtle to move a few steps, perhaps 20.

Whatever number you choose we will call *n*.

To draw a square you simply:

- Tell the turtle to walk forward *n* steps
- Tell the turtle to turn 90 degrees to the right
- Tell the turtle to walk forward *n* steps
- Tell the turtle to turn 90 degrees to the right

And so on, until the turtle has drawn four sides and turned four corners.

You could use left turns instead of right turns. It doesn't matter as long as you use the same sort of turn throughout the series of commands.

To draw a rectangle

Drawing a rectangle is like drawing a square. But instead of picking one number, you have to pick two numbers. You have to decide:

- how **tall** the rectangle is going to be
- how **wide** the rectangle is going to be

The rectangle could be tall and thin, or short and wide. It all depends on the two numbers you pick.

For now let's call the width of the rectangle *x*, and the height of the rectangle *y*. To draw a rectangle you have to type commands which tell the turtle to:

- Move forward *y* steps
- Turn 90 degrees
- Move forward *x* steps
- Turn 90 degrees

And so on, until the turtle has drawn all four sides and turned all four corners of the rectangle.

Logo commands in full *p87*

Drawing triangles ■

Triangles are trickier to draw than squares and rectangles. You need to make the turtle draw three lines, and turn three corners. But you have to make decisions about:

- the length of all three sides. They can all be the same, or they can all be different
- the number of degrees in each corner of the triangle.

You have to make sure that the turtle ends up at exactly the same place on the screen that it started.

Here is one pupil's first try at drawing a triangle. As you can see it didn't work out.
The turtle hasn't returned to where it started.

The commands the pupil gave

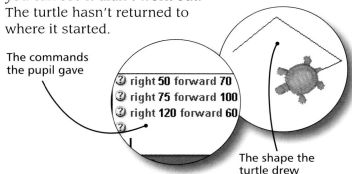

```
right 50 forward 70
right 75 forward 100
right 120 forward 60
```

The shape the turtle drew

The pupil has given commands to draw three lines and turn three corners, but the turtle hasn't arrived back where it started.

Next, the pupil gave the command **CS** (clearscreen) and tried again.

This time the result is much better. The turtle nearly draws a triangle, but not quite. The last corner needs to be a bit bigger, and the last side a bit longer.

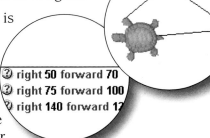

```
right 50 forward 70
right 75 forward 100
right 140 forward 1
```

On Target

You should now be able to:

- type in **Logo** computer commands
- spot and correct errors
- pick the right commands in the right order
- use repeat commands to produce regular geometric shapes.

This was the pupil's next try at drawing a triangle.

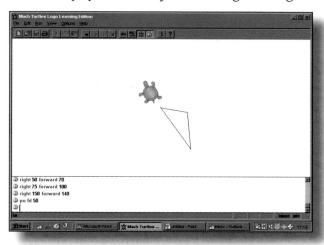

```
right 50 forward 70
right 75 forward 100
right 150 forward 140
pu fd 50
```

This time it worked! There are lots of different ways to draw a triangle, because there are lots of different types of triangle. It might take you more than three tries to get it completely right.

But don't worry – one of the good things about using the computer is that you can try as many times as you like. The computer won't get tired or fed up. It lets you explore as many changes and possibilities as you want.

WHAT YOU HAVE TO DO

1. **Give the commands which make the turtle draw a square. Print out the commands and the turtle's track.**

   If you have time draw several different squares of different sizes.

2. **Give the commands which make the turtle draw a rectangle. Print out the commands and the turtle's track.**

   If you have time draw several different rectangles of different sizes.

3. **Give the commands which make the turtle draw a triangle. Print out the commands and the turtle's track.**

   If you have time draw several different triangles of different shapes and sizes.

   Keep all your print-outs in your IT folder.

6

Searching for Information

Computers can be used to store information. In this unit you will learn how to use information stored on a computer to help you with your work.

On Target

In this unit you will learn how to use information stored on a computer.

You will learn:

- how to look at the information which is stored
- how to find the information that you want
- how to use the information when you find it.

CD-ROM

Computer systems are very good at helping you to look for information. The rest is still up to you!

A **CD-ROM** has a very high storage capacity. Companies produce CD-ROMs with lots of information stored on them.

To remind yourself about storage look on page 10.

Finding it Out for Yourself

In some of your lessons the teacher tells you everything you need to know. You need to listen, perhaps make notes, and remember.

But in other lessons you have to find things out for yourself. You have to look for the information.

This gives you more freedom, and more responsibility. **You** have to decide:

- *what* to investigate
- *what* questions to ask
- *where* to look for the information
- *which* information is reliable
- *when* you have enough information.

Types of Information

You can find many different types of information on a computer system:

- text information
- pictures, diagrams and maps
- sound clips
- videos and animations.

Destruction around the world

A storm surge is often more destructive than a hurricane's high winds. Surface water bulges beneath the storm's low pressure. Driven by the wind, the sea level rises, and battering waves crash inland. Whether by waves or by wind, hurricanes, also called cyclones or typhoons, can bring devastation. In 1970, more than half a million people died in a storm surge caused by a typhoon in Bangladesh. In 1992, Hurricane Andrew and the flooding caused by it resulted in more than 30 billion dollars in damage in Florida—the costliest natural disaster in United States history.

On the left is an example of a screen of information from a CD-ROM. It includes text, pictures and a video clip with sound.

Preparing to Search

Before you start to look for information it is a good idea to prepare. Before you begin, make sure you know what you are looking for.

Sometimes it can be a good idea to write it down. Write it as a topic, or perhaps as a question. Here are some notes which pupils made before they began to search for information.

What did the Romans eat, (food, recipes, method of cooking)

Find names of modern painters and examples of pictures. Note — must be this century.

Where to Search

Where you search depends on what CD-ROMs are available at your school, or in your local public library.

There are two types of CD-ROM which might be useful to you:

● specialised CD-ROMs about one topic of interest
● general CD-ROMs which store information on a range of topics (like an encyclopaedia).

Microsoft *Encarta* – a CD-ROM encyclopaedia

Looking Through a CD-ROM

When you start a CD-ROM it opens a window on the screen. The information in the CD-ROM is displayed on the screen in the window. You look at the information from a CD-ROM one screen at a time.

When you read a book you turn the pages. When you look through a CD-ROM you click on **links**. A link might be a button, a word, or a picture. When you click on the link you move to a different part of the CD-ROM.

Getting IT Right in...

History

You might be studying a topic such as *Warfare in the Middle Ages*. If you wanted to find out more about how castles were built, and how they protected the inhabitants in time of war, you could look on CD-ROMs and find pictures of castles.

You could also discover the names of different parts of the castle, and how the style of castle changed over time as building techniques improved.

WHAT YOU HAVE TO DO

For this unit you will need a topic or subject for investigation. If you aren't certain what subject to choose, pick one from this list:

■ **Animals of the rainforest**
■ **Jet powered flight**
■ **The Ancient Egyptians**
■ **Polar exploration**

Once you have decided on a topic, complete these tasks:

1. **Write out the topic you have chosen. Write a sentence or two about what information you want to find out.**

2. **Think of a specific question relating to your topic. Your task will be to find an answer to this question. Pick a question you don't already know the answer to. Check your question with your teacher.**

Keep these details in your IT folder.

I. Finding your way around

To begin with you will see how you can read through a CD-ROM. This involves being able to move from screen to screen and back again.

Navigating a CD-ROM

The information stored on a CD-ROM is organised into screens full of words, pictures and other items. On this page you will learn how to look through a CD-ROM, moving between the screens, and how to use the Contents.

Starting the CD-ROM ■

Often all you need to do to run a CD-ROM is to put it into the CD drive of your computer. It starts up automatically. Sometimes you have to use the Start menu, or a program icon.

Oceans ■

The example CD-ROM on this page is Microsoft *Oceans*. This is a CD-ROM that contains lots of pictures, videos, information and maps. The interface is quite complex, but it is carefully designed for you to find exactly what you want.

The interface ■

The **interface** is what lets you look through the CD-ROM. Every CD-ROM has a slightly different interface. Remember, the people who made the CD-ROM want it to be easy for you to use.

All CD-ROMs are organised in slightly different ways. This means you must pay careful attention to what you see on the screen. Make use of all the clues on the screen as these will help you to understand the CD-ROM.

On this page you will look at a particular example of a CD-ROM interface. The CD-ROMs you use at school are unlikely to be exactly the same as this one. However, look carefully at what you see on the screen. You should be able to find the same general features.

The screen you see when you start up the *Oceans* CD-ROM

The buttons along the bottom of the screen let you choose which part of the CD-ROM you want to look at

Navigation means finding your way around. The **navigation bar** is a series of buttons that you can click on to move to different sections of the CD-ROM. Four important features that you might find are:

- Home
- Back
- Next
- Help

Home

The **Home** screen is usually the first or main screen of the CD-ROM. From the Home screen you can get to any other part of the CD-ROM. At any time you can return to the Home screen from any place in the CD-ROM.

The *Contents* screen functions as a Home screen on the *Oceans* CD-ROM. Click on the *Contents* button to return to the start.

Back

A **link** will take you to a new screen. Clicking on the **Back** button will take you back to the screen you just left.

This button is useful if you make a mistake and follow a link to a screen that you don't want to look at. It is also useful when you have finished checking a screen and want to go back to where you were before.

Next

Sometimes a topic will cover several screens. Clicking on the **Next** button will take you to the next screen on the topic.

This button is useful if you want to follow a subject through several connected screens.

Some CD-ROMs have arrows instead of *forward* and *back*.

Help

Look out for a button that says **Help**. Clicking on this button will often display helpful advice on the screen.

Sometimes the Help advice is very good, sometimes not so good. It is always worth a try.

The **Contents** page of a book shows you the main topics of the book. It is not in alphabetical order. It is in the order that the subjects are organised. The Contents screen of a CD-ROM has the same function. It shows you the main sections of the CD-ROM.

Clicking on a topic heading on the Contents screen will take you to the start of that section.

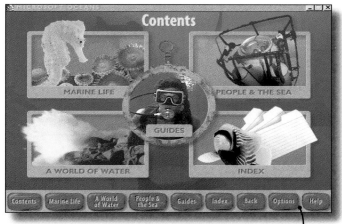

The Contents screen of the *Oceans* CD-ROM

Navigation buttons

The Contents screen offers you a number of different ways of looking at the CD-ROM. You will learn more about some of these options later. For now, just remember that you follow links by clicking on them to look at screens of data.

WHAT YOU HAVE TO DO

Load a CD-ROM. Look at the interface. Answer these questions.

1. **What is the name of the CD-ROM? What is the subject covered by the CD-ROM?**

2. **Does it have a Contents screen? List the main headings of the Contents screen.**

3. **Does it have a navigation bar? Or some other way of letting you navigate? List the navigation buttons.**

4. **What are your first impressions of the CD-ROM? Write a short review of it, advising other people of your age about whether it is easy or hard to use.**

Keep your work in your IT folder.

2. Desperately seeking...

On this page you will learn how to search through a CD-ROM for information on a particular topic.

Searching

On the last page you looked at ways to navigate a CD-ROM, clicking on links and using the navigation bar. This is a good way to look at a CD-ROM. It is the same as reading through a book.

But sometimes you have a particular subject in mind. You need to find out about a topic, or you need to find the answer to a question. Picking out the right information is called **searching**. CD-ROMs offer different techniques to help you to find the information.

On this page you will look at ways to find information on a CD-ROM. The *Oceans* CD-ROM is again used as an example.

Word search

On the *Oceans* CD-ROM the **word search** is linked to the Index. On other CD-ROMs the word search will look through the entire CD-ROM.

In any case, a word search will look for a **match**. If you type in a word or phrase the word search will look through until it finds a match for what you typed in.

If you are doing a **word search**, pick the word carefully. Be prepared to try a different word if the first search doesn't work.

Most importantly – make sure you spell the word properly!

Index

On the right is what you see when you click on the **Index** option from the **Contents** or the **navigation bar** of the *Oceans* CD-ROM.

The Index gives you an alphabetical list of topics.

Click on any letter to see the topics which start with that letter. On the *Oceans* CD-ROM there are eight topics starting with the letter A.

Click on the topic heading to see a screen of information on that topic.

On the next page you will see how to make good use of a screen of information when you find it.

Word search

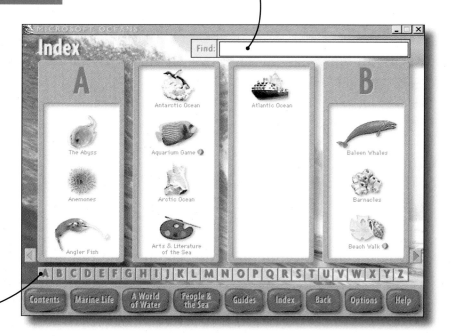

Pick a letter

Special features

Many CD-ROMs offer special features to help you find the topic you want. Of course these vary between different CD-ROMs. Look out for special features when you are searching for information on any CD-ROM.

CD-ROMs sometimes offer special features to help you. The *Oceans* CD-ROM offers a number of these special features. For example, the **Guides** feature.

This presents a number of (imaginary) people. You can pick the person you want. He she (or it) will present some of the information from the CD-ROM.

This is an interesting way to skim through a whole range of subjects.

Another special feature is called a **time-line**. Along the top is a series of time periods from ancient prehistory. Click on one of these eras and see the ocean life of that time.

The five major eras of prehistory are shown on this bar

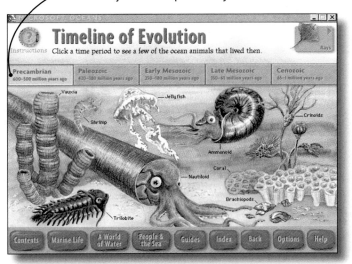

Here are some other special features you might find on a CD-ROM.

A map

The CD-ROM might include a map. Typically you can click on one area of the map to find out more information about that area.

A scene

There might be a picture of an outdoor scene. For example a CD about the animals of the rainforest might have a picture showing the various parts of the forest (the canopy, the undergrowth etc.). You could pick part of the scene to learn about the animals that live in that part of the forest.

A picture index

Here is a simple picture index from the *Oceans* CD-ROM. It shows a range of mammals that live in the ocean. Click on the picture of an animal to learn more.

WHAT YOU HAVE TO DO

On page 93, you chose a topic of interest and a question to investigate. Use the search facilities you have to see what you can discover.

Write notes about your search.

- **What did you do?**
- **What facilities did you use?**
- **Did you find what you wanted?**

Keep your work in your IT folder.

3. I've found it!

Here you will learn how to make good use of the information that you find on a CD-ROM.

Using what you find

You have learned how to look through a CD-ROM and how to search for information on a particular topic. But what do you do when you find the information you want?

On this page you will look at how information is presented on the screen when you use a CD-ROM. You will also look at the ways in which you can make use of the information to help with your work.

As before, the *Oceans* CD-ROM is used as an example.

Information

When you follow a link you will see a screen of information. This example shows information about *rays* (large fish related to sharks). The screen includes text and pictures. It also includes some other interesting features:

- **Quiz**. Click on this link for a short multiple choice quiz, with animation and sounds.

- **Remarkable Powers**. This is a link to the next screen. It explains some of the unusual things rays can do.

  The red words on the screen are links to other items.

- **A piece of film**. The piece of film shown on this link means that it leads to a short video clip. This clip shows human divers swimming with rays.

Highlighted words

Many of the words on the screen are **highlighted**. By clicking on any of the highlighted words you can call up further information on the subject. This is useful if, for example, you aren't sure what a word means.

Click on a highlighted word to see an explanation

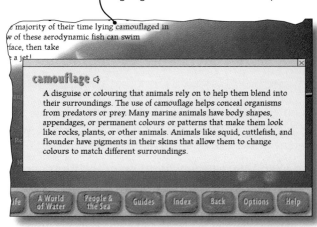

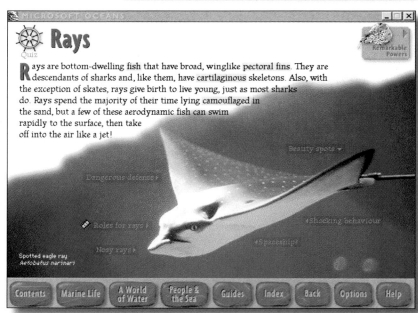

What to do with it ■

When you've found what you're looking for there are several things you can do with it.

Write it down

The easiest way to use the information is to simply note it down. Always have a pen and some paper handy when you look through a CD-ROM.

Copy and print

In some CD-ROMs you can select pictures and other items. You can **copy** them (put them onto the clipboard) and then **paste** them into your own documents. CD-ROMs like this often have menus that let you pick **copy** as an option. Look out for this.

In some CD-ROMs you can pick out screens, or parts of screens, and **print** them out. Again, look out for buttons or menus which give you this option.

The *Oceans* CD-ROM does not offer a lot of copy, paste and print options. However it does have a picture gallery of images that you can use.

Click here to see a list of available images

The bar at the bottom of the picture lets you print or copy the image. **Make Wallpaper** means that you can use the picture as background on the desktop screen of your computer.

The company has given you permission to make use of these pictures. Remember to always check for legal permission before you use pictures and other items.

Know all about IT

CD-ROMs in close-up

Information on a CD-ROM is stored using millions of microscopic holes. These are called **pits**. They are burned into the shiny surface.

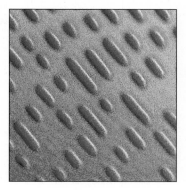

A laser beam reads them by shining its light onto the pits. The computer can detect the way the light is reflected back.

Because the pits are so tiny the CD-ROM can hold as much information as 250,000 pages of typed words. That's the same as about two thousand books as big as the one you are reading now!

IT at work

Many jobs involve finding things out. People use books and other paper-based materials to discover the information they need.

CD-ROMs might be used by:

- a teacher collecting text and pictures to use in a hand-out for pupils
- a journalist looking for background information for a magazine article
- a musician needing unusual music samples.

WHAT YOU HAVE TO DO

You have found information on your topic of interest on a CD-ROM.

- ■ **Use Copy or Print (or both) to extract text, pictures or other items from the CD-ROM. Check for copyright permission.**

Put the items you extracted into your IT folder.

4. On the record

On the final page of this unit you will learn about databases. You will be doing a lot more work with databases in Books 2 and 3.

Data structures

As well as looking at information from bought sources, such as CD-ROMs, you might want to look through data sources which have been prepared by teachers or other pupils at your school. For example:

- many schools have a Weather Centre where they record a range of measurements such as temperature and rainfall
- information stored for a class to use, such as historical facts and figures
- the results of surveys carried out by pupils.

Whatever the reason, you might need to:

- look at results stored on the computer
- add new results to those already stored.

A large collection of information stored on a computer is called a **Database**. There are standard rules for how databases are put together. In this section you will learn how databases are made, and look at some examples.

Databases

Databases are collections of information. The data is not stored all higgledy-piggledy. It is structured and arranged into **records** and **fields**. You will see what these are on this page.

This kind of data organisation existed before computers were invented. When you want to store data in a way that is easy to find you can use a card file. Some libraries still use this system so you might have come across it.

A card file holds a series of identical cards. Each card is laid out in the same way.

Here is an example of a card used in a library:

```
ROSWELL PUBLIC LIBRARY

TITLE      :     Terrible Tudors
Author     :     Terry Deary
Publisher  :     Scholastic Ltd
Subject    :     British History
Library Code:    R9/hh/a
ISBN       :     0 - 590- 19772 - X
```

These cards could be stored in an index box or a filing cabinet.

The structure of a computer database is very similar. Records represent the cards and fields represent the pieces of information on the cards.

Records

Each **record** in a database holds the information about one person or thing. In a library database one record holds all the information about one book. In a weather station database one record might hold all the information about the weather on one day.

A record in a database is equivalent to one card in a card file.

Fields

Each piece of information in a record is called a **field**. For example in the library database the title of the book is one field.

Every field has a **field name** and **contents**.

Subject : British History
Field name   Field contents

Every record in the database includes the same fields in the same order.

This is called the **database structure**.

Computer database

The simplest kind of computer database has one set of records. It is equivalent to one card file.

In some database programs you look at the records one at a time.

```
LIBRARY.DAT

RECORD NUMBER        0095

TITLE                Terrible Tudors

Author               Terry Deary

Publisher            Scholastic Ltd

Subject              British History

Library Code         R9/hh/a

ISBN                 0 - 590- 19772 - X
```

One record from the library database,
as displayed on a computer screen

Tables

In other database programs the records are arranged into a **table**.

Each **record** takes up one horizontal row of the table.

Each **field** takes up one column of the table.

Record No.	Title	Author	Publisher	Subject
0095	Terrible Tudors	Deary	Scholastic Ltd	History
0096	Murderous Maths	Poskitt	Scholastic Ltd	Maths
0097	Disgusting Digestion	Arnold	Scholastic Ltd	Biology
0098	Chemical Chaos	Arnold	Scholastic Ltd	Chemistry

Four records from the library database, arranged into a table

It is very easy to look through and you can see all the information on the screen.

A simple database like this can be set up and used with a spreadsheet package. There is more information about this on the next page.

On Target

You should now know how to:

- look at the information which is stored
- find the information that you want
- use the information when you find it.

WHAT YOU HAVE TO DO

How are records kept in your school library – with index cards or on a computer? Investigate the library at your school.

If the school uses a card index system then answer these questions:

1. How many collections of record cards are there?

2. What order are the cards in?

3. What information is on each card?

Keep your work in your IT folder.

7 On the Internet

The Internet is an exciting source of ideas and information. The key to using the Internet is finding the information you need quickly and easily. You also need to be sure the information is accurate and reliable.

On Target

In this unit you will learn:

- what the Internet is
- how to use Internet software
- how to search for information on the Internet
- how to make use of the information you find.

The Internet

The **Internet** is a system that connects together computers all over the world. Many computers are connected through telephone links. Nobody owns the Internet; it is a huge web of different types of computers and different kinds of links.

The Internet has grown up over the last two decades. It is still growing. It is impossible to say exactly how many people use the Internet nowadays. It is certainly many millions.

By using an Internet link you can take information directly from other computers. This information can be text, pictures or multimedia. You can:

- simply look at it
- copy it onto your own computer
- print it out
- use it in your own documents and presentations.

Much of this information is available free of charge.

Web Sites

Lots of people have computers that are connected to the Internet. Often these people want to share some of the information on their computer with other Internet users. They want other people to be able to read the text, look at the pictures and so on.

Nowadays the main way that people make these things available is through a **web site**. A web site is a collection of computer screen displays which is connected to the Internet.

People and organisations make web sites and then join them to the Internet so that anyone can look at them.

This is part of a web site set up by NASA, the American space agency

The World Wide Web

The collection of all the web sites in the world is called the **World Wide Web**, or **WWW**.

True or False?

Just because you find something on a web site, must it be true? Of course not: you have to use your judgement to decide this for yourself.

Anyone can put anything they like on a web site. It might be true, but it might not. You have the responsibility of judging for yourself.

In many countries (including the UK) there are laws which say that advertisements must be true, and that you can't tell lies about people (known as slander). Because the Internet isn't in any country, it is not covered properly by these laws.

In some ways this makes the Internet a very exciting place. But it also means you have to be careful when you use the Internet.

Trick or Treat?

People do put inaccurate information on web sites, for a joke or to trick you. Sometimes the tricks are obvious, and sometimes they are harder to spot. Compare what you see on a web site with what you read in the paper and see on TV.

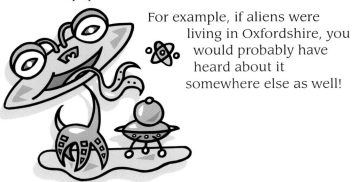

For example, if aliens were living in Oxfordshire, you would probably have heard about it somewhere else as well!

Advertisements

Some web sites are created by companies to tell you about their products. Remember they are trying to encourage you to buy them. Treat a product site on the Internet just like you would an advert on the TV. Sometimes you have to take adverts with a pinch of salt. Is the product really the best in the world?

Getting IT Right in...

Geography

You could search for sites on the Internet if you were studying volcanoes and earthquakes and their impact on communities. You might find pictures of volcanoes in the past, and information about volcano activity going on today.

Mistakes

People don't always mean to mislead, but they do make mistakes. Here is just one example: someone might believe they have a cure for the common cold and post it on their web site. They might be mistaken. Or perhaps they really have made a medical breakthrough.

For this reason, don't follow any advice which might be dangerous. Don't believe things without thinking about them first.

WHAT YOU HAVE TO DO

Make a list of the advantages and disadvantages of the Internet as a way of finding things out. How does it compare with other sources such as books, magazines, newspapers and TV?

Keep your work in your IT folder.

I. Just browsing

On this page you will learn how to use the software which lets you look at web sites. You will use the software to connect to a range of web sites, and to print them out to go in your folder.

Using a web browser

You have seen that a web site is a computer display that you can look at using the Internet. You can download web sites from all over the Internet and look at them on your computer at school or at home.

Web browsers

A **web browser** is a piece of software which lets you look at web sites. There are two main web browsers – **Netscape *Navigator*** and **Microsoft *Internet Explorer***. The makers of these two packages are great rivals. The packages are just as good as each other.

The windows of the two packages look slightly different, with different tool bar icons. But you can easily use either as you read this book.

This is the icon for Microsoft *Internet Explorer*.

Counting the cost

At school you are unlikely to be asked to pay to use the Internet. At home though, someone has to pay the telephone bill. Many Internet service providers also make extra charges over a certain number of hours, or for certain sites.

Make sure you always ask permission before dialling up the Internet.

Browser windows

The window of a web browser looks like this.

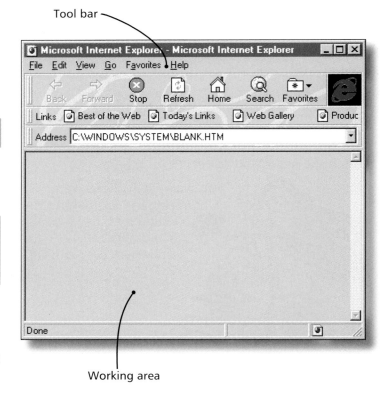

Tool bar

Working area

When you connect to a web site its contents will be displayed in the working area of the web browser. So, if you connected to the NASA site shown on the last page, you would see it displayed in the working area of your web browser.

Logging on

When you start up a web browser the computer will connect to the Internet. Depending on the system in place at your school you may have to **log on** to the Internet. You may have to give a name and password.

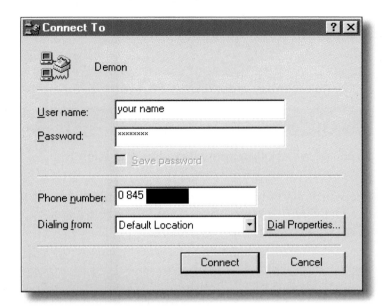

The computer has to connect to the Internet so that it can download web sites from other computers.

Using the Web address

Every web site in the World Wide Web has an address. The address is called the **URL** of the site. URL stands for **Uniform Resource Locator**. Say it by naming the letters (yoo – ar – el).

For example the URL of the NASA web site is:

http://www.nasa.gov

The URLs of web sites are sometimes given on the TV, or in magazines. Adverts often include the URL of the company web site. Look out for them.

(NB: sometimes URLs are shown without the starting letters http://)

visit www.popstar.com.uk
to keep up with the latest
hits in this country.
More for your favourites folder
Top Ten : www.music.com
Jokes : www.ukplus.co.uk
in the rest of the

Connecting to a web site

To use the URL of a web site, type it in at the top of the web browser window. Then press **Enter** .

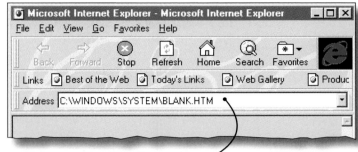

Type the URL here

The browser will look over the Internet for the web site. It might take a few seconds to find it. It might take a little longer to download it.

After a short wait you should see the web site in the working area of your web browser.

Have you tried...?

Here are some web addresses you might like to try:

www.beeb.com

A fun web site presenting information about BBC programmes.

www.beano.com

The web site for the BEANO comic.

www.yucky.com

A web site about science, from the point of view of the weird and the disgusting.

www.kidsdomain.com

A web site about computer games, with reviews and free demonstrations.

WHAT YOU HAVE TO DO

Make a collection of URLs by looking out for them on the TV and in magazines. Also note down the subject of the web site (for example, the company or TV programmme who set it up).

You will need these later. Keep your work in your IT folder.

2. Link up

You now know how to connect to web sites by using the addresses called URLs. On this page you will learn how to follow links to other web sites.

Links

Web sites have many interesting things on them: information, news, pictures, multimedia.

Web sites have one other interesting feature. They include **links** to other web sites. A link might be marked by words or by an icon for example. When you click on the link your browser loads a new web site.

A link might take you to a different part of the same web site. Or it might take you to a completely new web site, run by a different organisation. In this way you can move to a new web site without having to type a new URL.

On this page you will study an example taken from a real web site. The NASA web site was mentioned on the last page. One part of it is a gallery of free multimedia resources, all to do with space.

The URL for this part of the NASA site is:

http://www.nasa.gov/gallery/index.html

- Type this URL in your web browser

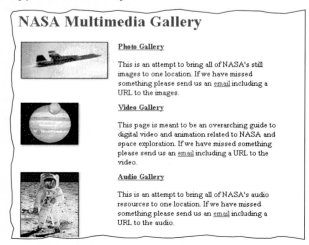

Find the link

Links are most often shown as <u>blue words</u> on the screen. They are usually underlined.

The words usually tell you what you are going to link to. This NASA site has three links: a <u>Photo Gallery</u>, a <u>Video Gallery</u> and an <u>Audio Gallery</u>.

Using the link

Links could not be easier to use. If you want to follow the link to a site then click on the link. Your web browser will immediately download the linked site.

- Click on the <u>Photo Gallery</u> link

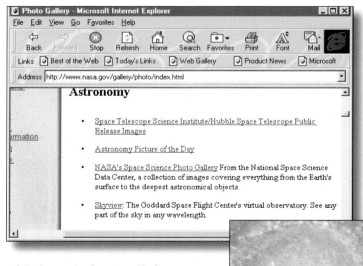

This is an index to all the astronomy photos on the NASA site. There are a number of links you can choose to follow.

- Click on <u>Astronomy Picture of the Day</u>

On 30 September 1998, this was the NASA 'Astronomy Picture of the Day'

Navigating

The web browser has tools on the tool bar that make it easy for you to move between sites.

You have followed a link. You are looking at a new site. Now you want to go back to the original site.

- Click on **Back** to go back to where you were before

By using **Forward** and **Back** you can swap between the two sites as often as you like

⇦ Back ⇨ Forward ✕ Stop

If you have followed several links you can click **Back** as often as you like, going back through all the sites you have looked at.

Stop

Sometimes a site takes a long time to download. Perhaps the connection is poor. Perhaps the site has lots of complicated pictures.

Sometimes you can tell that a site isn't what you want, even before it has finished downloading.

If you want to stop a site from downloading, for whatever reason, click on **Stop**.

Surfing

You download a site. It has links on it. You click on a link that looks interesting. A new site appears. The new site has more links. You click on one of these... and so on.

You can carry on like this, clicking on links and looking at new sites. This is called *Surfing the Internet*, or *Browsing the Web*.

Remember the rules of using the Internet wisely:

- be cautious about web site contents
- try not to get distracted from the task in hand.

To remind yourself about these points look back to page 103.

Link failure

Sometimes you type a URL or click on a link and it doesn't work. There are several reasons why this might happen:

- you have typed the URL wrongly – have another go
- the link you clicked on has been set up wrongly – there's not much you can do about this
- the site doesn't exist anymore. Web sites come and go
- the Internet is very busy and you can't make a connection.

It is probably worth trying again later to see if you can get through.

WHAT YOU HAVE TO DO

Work away from the computer.

1. **Take a web site print-out and mark with a pen each of the links shown on the site. This might be easiest with a coloured print-out.**

Work on the computer.

2. **When you are connected to a web site, click on a link to move to a new site. Try to follow a series of links, through three or four different sites.**

3. **Write notes about the sites that you found.**

You can use the NASA example from this page.

Keep your work in your IT folder.

3. Really useful engines

On this page you will learn how to use a search engine to find sites of interest.

Search engines

So far you have learned two ways to connect your web browser to a web site so that you can look at it:

- you can type the URL
- you can click on a link.

But you might not know the URL that you need. There are millions of web sites on the World Wide Web – nobody really knows how many. Whatever your topic of interest there are probably lots of sites which would be useful and interesting.

The trick is to find the right sites.

Luckily there is special software to help you to find the sites you need. This software is called a **search engine**. There are lots of search engines you can use.

Using a search engine

Search engines are computer programs that find web sites for you.

The search engine you use is not held on your computer at school. Instead search engines are held on their own web sites.

To use a search engine:

- start up the web browser
- connect to the Internet
- type the URL of the search engine.

You don't have to pay to use a search engine. They are usually provided by companies that have other software packages to sell.

Finding a search engine

There is a button on the tool bar of your web browser which looks something like this:

When you click on this button you will download a web site which lets you use one or more search engines. You might see a web site that looks something like this.

This web site lets you use four different search engines:
Excite
WebCrawler
Yahoo
Lycos

i Searching *p92*

AltaVista

One of the most popular search engines is called **AltaVista**.

The URL for the AltaVista web site is:

www.altavista.com

- Type this URL in your web browser to connect to the AltaVista web site

A web browser displaying the AltaVista web site

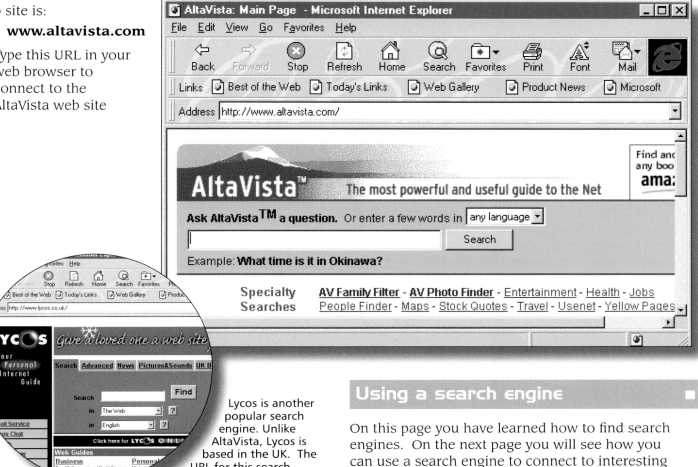

Lycos is another popular search engine. Unlike AltaVista, Lycos is based in the UK. The URL for this search engine is **www.lycos.co.uk**

Using a search engine

On this page you have learned how to find search engines. On the next page you will see how you can use a search engine to connect to interesting web sites.

WHAT YOU HAVE TO DO

1. Find the web sites of some search engines:
   - use the search tool on the tool bar
   - type the AltaVista URL into your web browser
   - find out about other search engines.
2. When you find the web site of a search engine, print out the web site contents.

Keep a record in your IT folder of all the web sites you have visited. Which one looks easiest to use?

4. Dinomaniac search (I)

On the previous page you learned how to connect with a search engine web site. On the following pages you will see how you can use a search engine to find the web sites you need for your school work.

Searching for sites

Picking the right **key words** is important if you are going to find the sort of information you are looking for.

Over the next few pages you can study one pupil's search. You can see how she used the search engine and the sites which she found.

Using a search engine ■

Search engines find web sites for you. They work by using **key words**.

To find web sites on a particular topic you must first:

● be clear about the topic you are interested in

● think of two or three key words on that topic

● type the key words into a search engine.

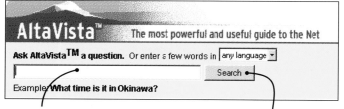

Type key words here   Click here to begin the search

Here are some tips to help you pick a good set of key words.

● Pick words that relate closely to your chosen topic.

● Pick words that are precise in meaning rather than vague words.

● Pick names (of people places and things).

● Spell the words correctly.

Picking key words ■

A search engine doesn't use a simple word search. A site doesn't have to contain all your key words. The search engine will find sites that contain just one of your key words. It might find thousands of sites. But it will only display a few sites on the screen at one time.

The sites it displays first are the sites that contain most of the key words. This shows you how important key words are. Pick them very carefully.

One problem you might find is that key words can have more than one meaning. A pupil was trying to find out about stars. She typed **stars** as a key word. Here are some of the sites the search engine found.

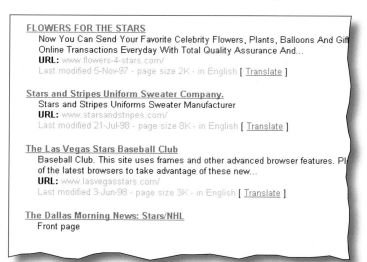

The problem is that **stars** is a word with so many different uses. She tried again, this time giving a series of key words (**star**, **astronomy**, **space**) and the search worked much better.

A pupil wanted to find web sites on the subject of *dinosaurs*. She particularly wanted to find some pictures.

She chose these key words:

- dinosaur
- extinct
- picture
- image

She typed them into the **AltaVista** search engine. It took a second or two for the search. Then the screen changed.

This is what she saw on the screen.

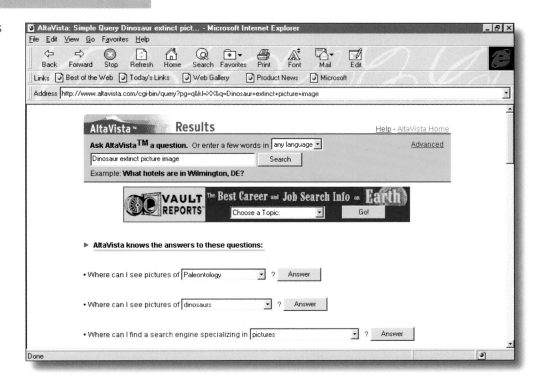

The AltaVista search engine is a clever one. It has picked out some answers that she might be interested in. Like *Where can I see pictures of Dinosaurs?* It has even suggested another topic she might be interested in – *Palaeontology*, the study of ancient life.

One action the pupil could take next is to click on one of the **Answer** buttons on the screen.

The search engine found nearly a million web pages

These are links to other web sites

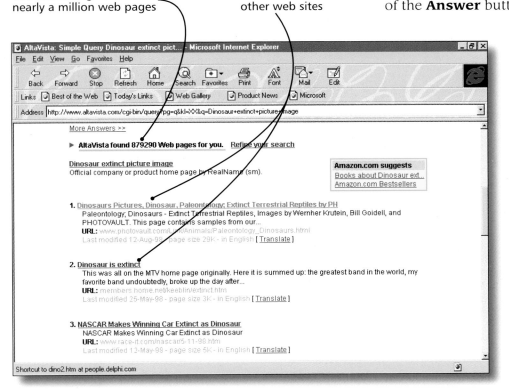

Let's look at what else the AltaVista search engine has found. By clicking on the scroll bar you can look further down the page.

The search engine says it found over 800,000 sites. But don't worry – the first few sites that it lists are usually the most useful ones.

The <u>blue words</u> on the screen are **links** to other web sites.

Not all the sites are useful ones. Link 2 seems to be about a rock band called *Dinosaur*!

5. Dinomaniac search (2)

There are even more links lower down the page.

You could carry on looking at pages of links. But there is no need.

Link 8 is to the *DINOMANIAC* page for people who are mad about dinosaurs. Sounds interesting!

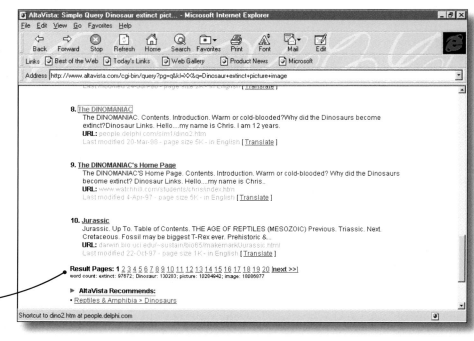

Click here for more pages of links

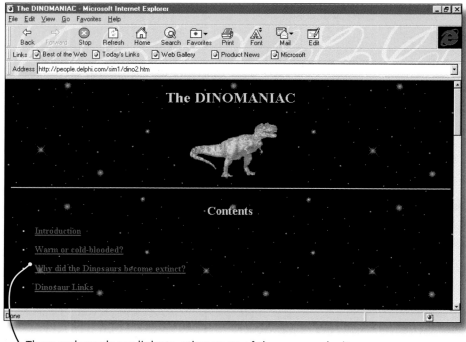

These red words are links to other parts of the same web site

The pupil clicked on this link and her web browser showed her the *DINOMANIAC* page. It looks like this.

There is much more on this web site. You can use the scroll bar to look through it, or click on the red links to see answers to particular questions – like *Were dinosaurs warm or cold-blooded?*

At the end of the web site is a section called *Dinosaur Links*. This is a section with links to other interesting dinosaur sites.

The pupil could follow some more of these links and see more dinosaur sites.

E-mail *p116*

The person who set up the *DINOMANIAC* site is interested in receiving **e-mail**.

E-mail is covered in Unit 8. The pupil could click on the *E-MAIL* notice at the bottom of the page to send a message to this person.

There is plenty more for the pupil to look at. She could:

- look at some of the *answers* to *questions* on the AltaVista page
- follow up some of the *other sites* found by AltaVista
- read the *DINOMANIAC* site carefully, because it looks interesting
- follow some of the links on the *DINOMANIAC* site.

This should have given you some idea of how much you can get from the Internet, and how easy it can be.

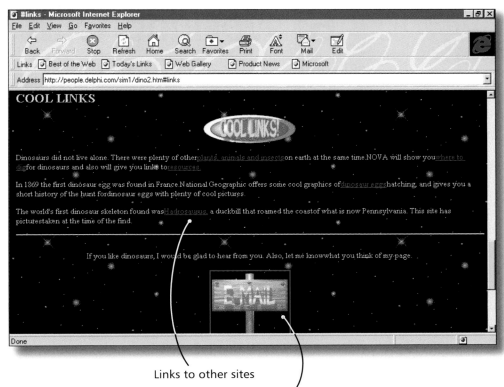

Links to other sites

Click here to send an e-mail to the site owner

IT at work

A Health Visitor is a trained nurse whose job is to visit people in her area. For example she will visit mothers of young children, and give them advice about such questions as vaccinations and appropriate feeding.

Sometimes a new health question arises very quickly. For example there might be a scare about a certain food – is it safe for young children? Lots of people will ask the Health Visitor's advice about this question. But there might not be very much information in medical textbooks and journals because it is such a new question.

The Internet is a good source of new information. The Health Visitor could quickly search the Internet to find out what medical opinion was, in the UK and in other countries too. But of course she would take care what web sites she looked at. If the information was published by a reliable source she could use it to help her with her job.

WHAT YOU HAVE TO DO

Carry out a search for web sites to find the following:

- **pictures of dinosaurs**
- **a description or pictures of a volcano erupting**
- **a site for fans of Sherlock Holmes, or another fictional character you know of.**

1. **Work away from the computer.**

   Work out the exact subject of your Internet search – what do you hope to find? Pick three or four key words for the search.

2. **Work on the computer.**

   Use the key words in a search engine to find sites.

There is more detail on the next page about how to make use of web sites that you find. For now, note down any interesting facts. Ask if you can use the Print tool to print out some of the sites you find.

6. Working with web sites

What should you do when you have found a useful site? There are lots of possibilities, as you will discover on this last page of this unit.

Using what you find

Once you've found a site with some useful information on it there are a number of things you can do, such as:

- making notes
- printing it out
- saving it
- copying particular items
- bookmarking it.

Make notes

Perhaps the easiest thing you can do when you find a web site is to make **notes**. Read what it says on the screen. Write down the facts which are going to be useful to you.

For example, below is what it says on the *DINOMANIAC* site about the extinction of the dinosaurs.

You could use this information in a project on the dinosaurs. But remember – just because something is on a web site, it might not be true. The *DINOMANIAC* site is a good one, but others may not be so accurate.

To remind yourself about web sites that can be wrong, turn back to page 103.

Print/Save/Open

You can print out a web site by clicking on this icon on the tool bar.

- Some sites print out better than others.
- Some sites will take a long time to print out, and use up a lot of paper or ink.
- Always ask permission before printing out a web site.

You can save the whole site as a file. Use the **File** menu.

Save the web site as a file ⟋ Open a file which you saved earlier

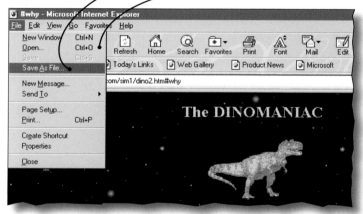

You can open the web sites you have saved and look at them using your web browser. You use **Open** just like opening a document file with a word processor.

Why did the Dinosaurs become extinct?

At the end of the Cretaceous Period, dinosaurs seem to have suddenly died out. So far scientists do not know why. This was a period continental drift, mountain building, changing plant life and weather. Some scientists believe a disease may have been the cause of th extinction, others believe that the dinosaur's food supply ran out as it was replaced with new plants that the dinosaurs could not adap Another theory is that a giant meteor struck the earth, causing a huge dust cloud which blocked the sun's rays - placing the earth into darkness, killing off much of the existing life.
Did all the dinosaurs die off leaving no direct decendents? It doesn't seem likely, and this view is now being closely examined by paleontologists and evolutionary biologists.

Sometimes you want to save or print just one item, not the whole web site. You might want to save just a picture taken from the page.

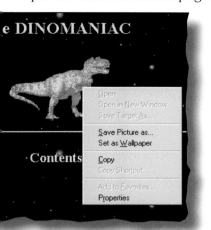

● Right-click on a particular item like a picture to select it

You will see this menu. There are some interesting choices on this menu. You can save the picture as a file on your computer. You can also **Copy** the picture. You could then **Paste** it, for example into a word processed document.

Remember that **copyright** is an issue. Just because something is on a web site doesn't mean you can use it in any way you like.

Most people would not mind a school pupil copying a picture into a work project. However some commercial sites are very sensitive about any copying. If in doubt, send an e-mail to the site owner.

Note the URL ■

If you find a site you like you can write down the **URL** (the address of the site) in your notebook. The URL is shown at the top of the web browser.

Remember that you can type a URL into a web browser and the browser will find the site and download it. But be careful of typing errors. If you leave out a single punctuation mark in a URL it won't work.

On Target

In this unit you should have learned:

- what the Internet is
- how to use Internet software
- how to search for information on the Internet
- how to make use of the information you find.

If you are reading a book, and you have to stop, you sometimes put in a bookmark. When you come back to the book later the bookmark will let you go back to the same page.

You can **bookmark** a favourite web site like this.

If you are using the Internet and you find a site you like, it can be frustrating when the end of the lesson comes and you have to close down the computer. Will you ever find that site again?

● Before you stop work, click on this icon

The bookmark menu looks like this.

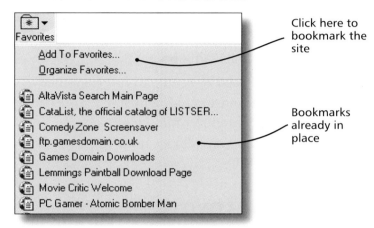

Click here to bookmark the site

Bookmarks already in place

● Click on **Add To Favorites**

A bookmark to the site will be added to the list.

You can click on any of the bookmarks in the list and the web browser will take you directly to that site.

WHAT YOU HAVE TO DO

You have found web sites relating to a topic of interest. Return to these web sites now.

1. **Write down the URL of each site.**

2. **Write some notes from at least one site, and type these up as a word processed document.**

3. **Print out at least one of the sites.**

4. **Save at least one of the sites.**

5. **Copy a picture from a site and paste it into the document you made.**

6. **Bookmark the best sites you found.**

8 Electronic Mail

E-mail is a way of sending messages using computer links. In this unit you will learn how to send e-mail messages, and to read e-mail sent to you.

On Target

In this unit you will learn about:

- the software used to send and receive e-mail
- how to write and send an e-mail
- how to send computer files by e-mail
- how to build up an address book full of e-mail addresses.

E-mail Software

There are a number of different e-mail packages. The example used in this section is **Microsoft Internet Mail**. Other packages may look slightly different, but they operate in much the same way.

In some older packages the functions are not shown as tool bar icons. They are held on menus instead. Look though the menus to find the functions that you need.

What is E-mail?

E-mail is short for **Electronic Mail**. It is just what the name says – mail (letters) sent in an electronic form. E-mail is sent to your computer down a telephone line.

With e-mail you can write a letter to anywhere in the world, and have it delivered in a few minutes. Along with your e-mail you can send any computer file. This might be a picture, or an essay, or data in a spreadsheet.

The person you have sent the e-mail to will be able to download the e-mail and read it. Unlike a phone call, they don't have to answer as soon as you send the e-mail. They can wait until they have a free moment and then check how many e-mails they have waiting for them.

If you receive an e-mail it is very easy to reply to the person who sent it, or to **forward** the message to another of your friends to look at.

Everyone who has an e-mail account has an e-mail address that is unique to that account. You may have an e-mail account of your own through the school system. Or perhaps your class has a single e-mail account and you all share that address.

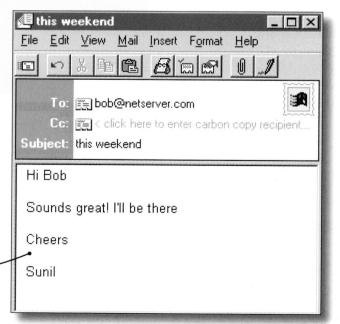

This is the text of the e-mail message

Writing E-mails

E-mail is usually a lot less formal and structured than letters sent through the post. Because it only takes a few seconds to write and send, people tend to be a bit more casual and relaxed.

Using *smileys*

When people read e-mails they can't see the writer's face. How can they tell if they are speaking seriously or just making a joke? A lot of people put little pictures of faces into their e-mails, to show whether they are happy, joking, sad, confused or whatever.

The little pictures are made up of punctuation marks on the computer keyboard. They are sometimes called **smileys** or **emoticons**. Here are some common smileys. To understand them, turn the page sideways.

> :-) I am happy/joking
>
> :-(I am sad/apologising
>
> :-0 I am surprised

Keeping it short

It is also common to use abbreviations, such as:

> IMHO In My Humble Opinion
>
> ROFL Rolling On the Floor Laughing
>
> BTW By The Way

Getting IT Right in...

Religious Education

Some pupils were studying prayers that were important to people from different religious groups. Their teacher gave them the e-mail addresses of information services for several religious organisations. Each pupil wrote an e-mail to a different organisation. Most of them wrote back with the words of a well loved prayer. The pupils put all of these together to make a display in the school library.

Knowing the Jargon

There are a few jargon words invented by e-mail users. These three describe bad behaviour on the Internet.

- **Spamming** – sending *junk* e-mails. Like junk mail, these are usually adverts. Like junk mail, spam e-mail usually gets on your nerves.
- **Flaming** – sending *insulting* e-mails. Because you can't see the person sending an e-mail, it is particularly important to avoid flaming.
- **Trolling** – being annoying on purpose to provoke flaming. Some people just like to provoke a row. The best response to trolling is to ignore it.

WHAT YOU HAVE TO DO

1. Imagine you want to invite a group of friends to a party. You could do it by phone, by sending a letter, or by using e-mail. How might e-mail be better than phoning or writing? How might it be worse?

2. Make a list of the advantages and disadvantages of using e-mail as a way to send messages.

Keep your work in your IT folder.

I. Where it's @

First you will learn about e-mail addresses and the special features of e-mails, such as quoting and attachments.

What's so special about e-mail?

An e-mail is very different from an ordinary letter. For a start it gets there much quicker. There are also special features that make e-mails particularly useful. You can automatically quote an e-mail back to the person who sent it to you, or automatically forward it to a third person. You can attach computer files to an e-mail and send them through the e-mail connection to anyone anywhere in the world.

E-mail addresses are different from normal addresses and phone numbers. On this page you will learn how to use e-mail addresses. You need to start noticing and noting down e-mail addresses.

Addresses

People will tell you their e-mail addresses. You see them on adverts and in magazines. Radio DJs and TV presenters often give out e-mail addresses. You will also find e-mail addresses on the Internet.

E-mail addresses typically look like this:

andy.parsnip@dodgy.co.uk

The name of the person ⌐ ⌐ Their organisation or the e-mail server that they use

To *say* an e-mail address out loud you say **dot** for the **full stops** and **at** when you see the symbol @. So the address here would be pronounced:

Andy dot Parsnip at Dodgy dot Co dot UK

You have probably heard people say e-mail addresses in this way.

Know all about IT

An e-mail account is typically connected to the Internet through a server. The server is a computer that is connected permanently to the Internet by a communications link.

When you send an e-mail message to a person it is sent to that person's server and stored there. When the person is ready to look at their e-mails they link their computer to the server – perhaps by a phone link – and the server sends them all the stored messages.

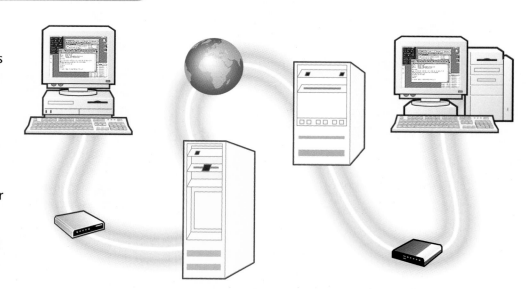

 Keyboards *p52*   Replying to and attaching files *p126*

Quoting

In many e-mail systems the computer will automatically generate a reply to any e-mail you receive. This reply is automatically addressed to the person who sent you the e-mail. It often **quotes** the message you received. For example if Bob replied to Sunil's e-mail (see the example below) his reply would look like this before he had even typed anything:

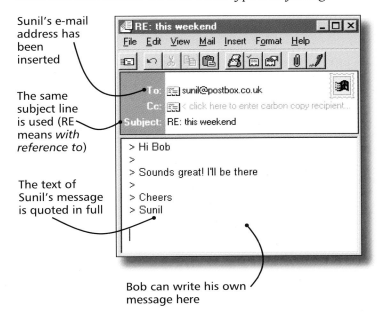

Sunil's e-mail address has been inserted

The same subject line is used (RE means *with reference to*)

The text of Sunil's message is quoted in full

Bob can write his own message here

Bob can now write a reply to Sunil in the space at the bottom of the e-mail.

If the e-mail you are replying to is long, it is good practice to delete most of the quoted text. Only leave the lines that are relevant to your reply. Otherwise e-mails can get very long and hard to read.

Attachments

You can **attach** any computer file to an e-mail.

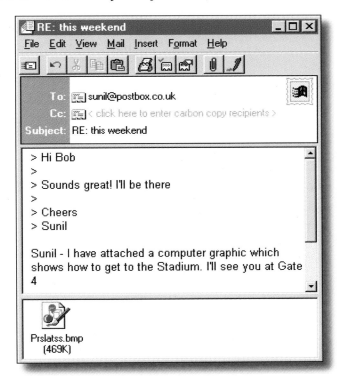

In the example above Bob has attached a graphic file to the e-mail. When he sends the e-mail the file will be sent along too. When he receives the e-mail Sunil can open the file and use it just like any other file on his computer system, if he has the same program.

The only disadvantage of attaching files with pictures to e-mails is that it can take several minutes to send them down the telephone line.

There's more on replying to and attaching files on page 126.

Directory enquiries

What happens if you want to send an e-mail to someone but you don't know their electronic address? You could start by searching one of the following web sites:

http://www.howhere.com

http://okra.ucr.edu/okra

http://www.four11.com

You will need to use some key words for your search. Some you try may be mainly American; some may be from other countries.

WHAT YOU HAVE TO DO

1. **Do you have an e-mail address at school? Is it just for you or for the whole class? Make a note of it in your IT folder.**

2. **Look (and listen) out for e-mail addresses. Make a list of e-mail addresses taken from magazines, radio and TV shows, and from friends with e-mail accounts. Keep the list in your IT folder.**

2. Packaging and posting

Next you will take a look at a typical e-mail package. This will help you get familiar with it before you start sending and receiving e-mail yourself.

A typical e-mail package

A typical e-mail package can be used for several different tasks. People might send e-mail to you. You can use the e-mail package to download it and read it. You can write your own e-mails and send them.

On the next few pages you will learn about some other e-mail actions.

Your e-mail package probably organises the messages using folders. It probably has a tool bar with a number of icons.

Folders

The e-mails that you send and receive are stored in four **folders**:

- Inbox
- Outbox
- Sent Items
- Deleted Items

Click on any folder to see its contents

The window

Here is the main window for Microsoft *Internet Mail*. It has all the familiar Windows features.

Menu bar   Tool bar   The working area is in two halves

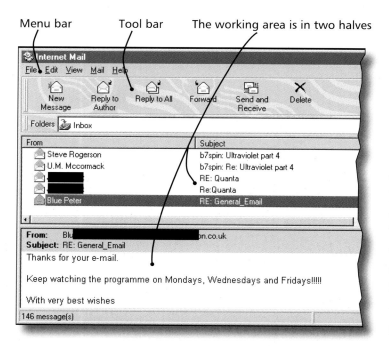

Inbox

The **Inbox** folder is used to store all the messages that people have sent to you.

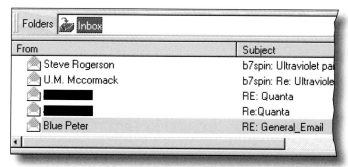

The window shows the names of all the people who have sent e-mails to you. It also shows the subject of each e-mail. It might also show the time and day when the message was received.

The list is usually sorted in order of when the message was received. The most recent messages are shown at the bottom of the list.

You will find out how to get into the Inbox, and how to read your e-mails, on page 124.

Outbox

The **Outbox** stores the e-mails you have written and are ready to send. You can read them and check them before they are sent.

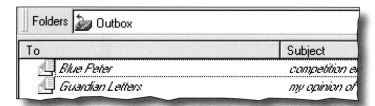

You should be aware that some computers have a permanent link to the Internet. On these computers e-mails may not be stored in an Outbox. They might be sent straight away. If your computer works this way you won't have a chance to check your e-mails – so be extra careful!

Sent items

After you have sent an e-mail a copy is stored in the **Sent Items** folder. You can look back to remind yourself of what e-mails you have sent.

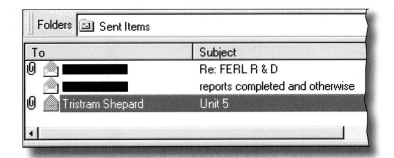

Deleted items

You can delete any of the e-mails in any of your folders.

● Click on this icon

✕
Delete

Deleted e-mails are moved to the **Deleted Items** folder. You can still read them, reply to them, or whatever you want. But if you delete them from this folder they will be removed for good.

The working area

The working area is divided into two parts.

This lists the e-mails stored in the folder

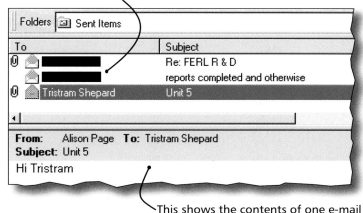

This shows the contents of one e-mail

One e-mail in the list is highlighted. It is usually the last one. You can see part of this e-mail in the window.

If you double-click on an e-mail it will open up in its own window. You can then read it. You will learn more about this on the next few pages.

Return to sender

What happens if you send an e-mail to an address that doesn't exist? Or maybe the person you sent it to has changed their e-mail address?

If this happens you will get a message back in your Inbox called **Undelivered Mail**, or something similar.

WHAT YOU HAVE TO DO

Write answers to these questions:

1. **What is the name of the software package used for e-mail on your school computer system?**

2. **What folders are there to hold the e-mail?**

3. **Pick one of the folders. What information is listed about each e-mail in this folder?**

4. **List the contents of the folder (if there are lots of e-mails in the folder, just list the ten most recent).**

3. Dear...

On this page you will learn how to prepare and send e-mail. It's very important to think carefully about what you say and the way that you say it.

Sending an e-mail

The best way to make sure you receive e-mail is to send e-mail. The more e-mail you send the more likely you are to get a reply.

Here are some reasons why you might send an e-mail:

- to friends as an alternative to making arrangements by phone
- to send your work to your teacher as a computer file
- to send fan mail and comments to your favourite TV programme (or band, football club, or whatever your interests are)
- to find things out and ask questions to help with projects.

Security matters!

- You should **never** include your age, home address or telephone number in an e-mail.
- Your school fax or telephone number should only be given with the permission of your teacher.
- Your parents must give your teacher their permission before you include a photograph of yourself with an e-mail.

New message

- Click on this icon on the tool bar to open a blank window, ready to type a new e-mail message

You will see a new window, like this:

Enter the address here

Enter the subject here

Enter the text here

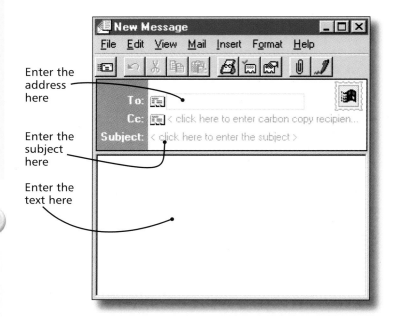

Address

- Enter the address of the person you want to write to

Subject

- Summarise the content of your message in a short phrase

Text

- Enter the text of your message

Netiquette

An e-mail is a lot quicker and easier to send than a letter. You can dash one off and send it in just a few seconds. Unlike a phone call you don't have direct contact with the person you are *talking* to.

These two features mean that it is very easy to give the wrong impression in an e-mail. It is important to be very careful not to cause unnecessary offence or say something that you will regret.

Here are some **netiquette** guidelines. Follow these rules to avoid problems.

- Never pass on anyone's e-mail address or the contents of an e-mail without permission.
- Never send an e-mail when you are feeling irritated. Write it if you must, and then leave it in your Outbox for a few hours until you cool off. Then read it again and make sure you haven't expressed yourself badly or in an offensive way.
- Never make comments about another person's beliefs or the country they come from – remember e-mail can go all over the world, so you must behave politely to people from all countries.
- If you mean a comment as a joke, you have to make it obvious. The people reading the e-mail can't tell that you are smiling when you send it. Say *this is just a joke* if you think it isn't clear.
- Don't send e-mail unless you are sure the person will be happy to receive it. Some people get hundreds of e-mails every day.

Into the Outbox

- Once you have entered all the items which make up your e-mail, click on this icon to send it to the **Outbox**

Writing off-line

Remember, you don't have to be connected to the Internet while you write your messages, only when you send them.

Save your phone bill by drafting and checking your messages **off-line**.

Send and Receive

- Click on the **Send and Receive** icon to send the e-mail

You may have to log on to the Internet server, giving your name and password.

The computer will send your e-mail down the phone line to the address you have given. In many packages, copies of all e-mails you send are stored in the **Sent Items** folder.

The computer will also look for any e-mail messages that are waiting for you on the Internet server. They will be copied onto your computer.

WHAT YOU HAVE TO DO

1. **Arrange with a partner to send an e-mail to one another. Make sure you know your partner's e-mail address.**

2. **Pick one or more of these suggestions:**

   - **Write a letter to a paper or magazine that you read. Use e-mail to send it. Newspapers often like you to include your postal address in the text of an e-mail.**

   - **Write a fan letter to someone or something that you like – a pop star, a TV programme or whatever.**

   - **Send an e-mail to someone in your family or among your friends who has an e-mail account. Tell them you have an e-mail account at school and ask them to reply.**

3. **When you have finished look in the Sent Items folder for the e-mail that you sent.**

4. Open the box

Here you will learn how to read e-mails, and how to make an e-mail address book.

Reading e-mail

Now that you have started to send e-mail it shouldn't be long before you get some replies.

You can read each e-mail that is sent to you. You can print it out or save it as a file on your computer.

You can also take the e-mail address from any e-mail that is sent to you. You can use these addresses to start to build up an address book of e-mail contacts.

Send and Receive

On the last page you saw how to use *Send and Receive*. When you use this command the computer:

● **sends out** any e-mails you have written
● **downloads** any e-mails sent to you.

You can use *Send and Receive* at any time. It might be a good idea to check once a day, or once a week, to see if you have been sent any e-mail.

Inbox

The **Inbox** folder is used to store all the messages that people have sent to you.

The window shows the names of all the people who have sent e-mails. It also shows the subject of each e-mail. It might also show the time and day when the message was received.

The list is usually sorted in order of when the message was received. The most recent messages are shown at the bottom of the list.

Reading the message

● Pick one of the e-mails in the Inbox and double-click on it to open it up

Who sent the message

> **[B7L] HORIZON NEWSFLASH**
> File Edit View Mail Help
>
> **From:** JMR
> **Date:** 16 November 1998 21:38
> **To:** blakes7@lysator.liu.se
> **Subject:** [B7L] HORIZON NEWSFLASH
>
> HORIZON AND AVON CLUB NEWSFLASH - Monday 16th November
>
> PAUL DARROW - yes, it's confirmed - The Avon Club and Horizon are delighted to announce that Paul WILL be returning to star as Captain Samuel Vimes in a 1999 UK tour of Terry Pratchett's GUARDS! GUARDS!
>
> Confirmed tour dates are: Opening 18/21 January 99, then also the week

The full text of the message

The window shows you:

● who sent the message and when
● who it was sent to (usually your e-mail address)
● the subject of the message
● the full text of the message.

Save

A button on the tool bar will let you save the e-mail as a separate computer file. However your e-mails will be kept in the **Inbox** until you decide to delete them, so you don't have to save them at once.

Print

As well as saving your e-mail, you can print it out to keep in your IT folder.

- Double-click on any of the entries in the **Sent Items** folder to look back at the e-mails you have sent

Save

Print

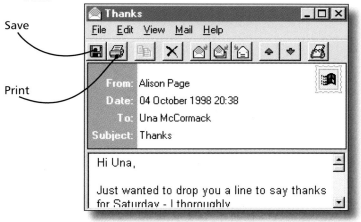

Using the address book

Many e-mail packages will let you create an **address book** of e-mail addresses. Type in new addresses as you learn them.

Part of an address book is shown below.

Click here to add an address to the list

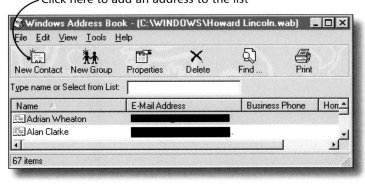

When you send an e-mail you can use an address from the address book. You can take the address out of the address book.

In this package, you click here to get an address from the address book

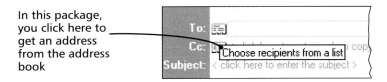

- Look through the address book for the name you want. Pick the right name by clicking on it

The computer will put the address into the e-mail.

Taking the address from an e-mail

When you receive an e-mail you can automatically add the address to the address book. In the package shown you right-click on the address and select **Add To Address Book**.

Pick this option from the menu

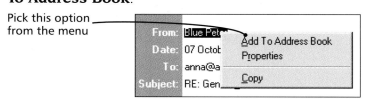

The computer automatically creates an address book entry.

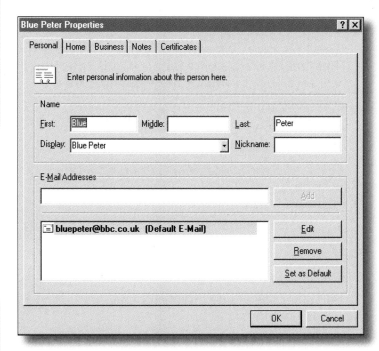

WHAT YOU HAVE TO DO

With luck, by now you will have received some e-mail messages in reply to those you sent.

1. **Put the address of each person who sent you an e-mail into the e-mail address book.**

2. **Write a list of the e-mail messages you have received. Write the name, subject and date of each message.**

3. **Print out each message you have sent or received.**

Put the list and the printed out messages into your IT folder.

5. Becoming attached

On the last page of this unit you will explore some of the special features of e-mail packages.

More work with e-mail

E-mail packages include a lot of extra features. These make work a bit easier. On this page you will learn about some of these e-mail extras:

- replying to e-mails you have been sent
- sending one e-mail to lots of people
- attaching a file to an e-mail.

Again, Microsoft *Internet Mail* is used as an example but all e-mail packages have similar features.

Reply

- Click on this icon to **reply** to an e-mail

The computer will create a reply for you. The original letter is quoted.

You can add your own text. To remind yourself about replying to e-mails look on page 119.

Multiple copies

You can send an e-mail to as many people as you like. Simply enter additional addresses at the top of the e-mail before you send it.

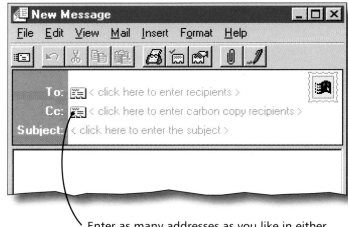

Enter as many addresses as you like in either the **To:** or **Cc:** sections of the e-mail

The address for your reply

The subject

The e-mail you are replying to is quoted here

Add your own text underneath

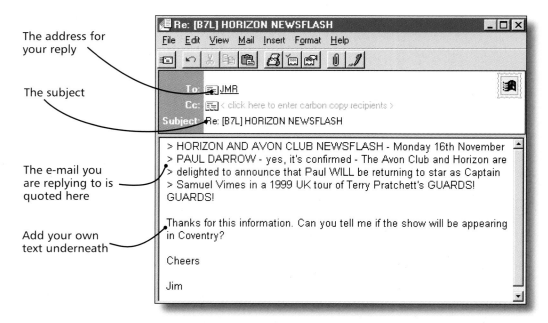

Special features of *Reply*

- The reply is automatically addressed to the person who sent the original e-mail.
- The subject of the original e-mail is shown, preceded with the letters Re:
- The original e-mail is quoted in full. Each quoted line starts with a >.
- You can delete the quoted lines.
- You can type new text.

Send e-mail *p122*

Forward

You can **forward** any e-mail that you receive. This means that you send it on to another friend to look at.

● Click on this icon to forward an e-mail

The computer generates an e-mail like this.

Add the address here

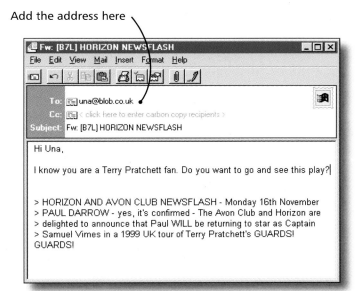

Special features of *Forward*

● You have to add an address to the message.
● The subject of the original e-mail is shown, preceded with the letters Fw:
● The original e-mail is quoted in full. Each quoted line starts with a >.
● You can delete the quoted lines.
● You can type new text.

It is generally bad manners to forward an e-mail without permission. Use your common sense – is the e-mail private or embarrassing? If so, it is better not to share it with anyone else.

On Target

You should now know how to:

■ use the software to send and receive e-mails
■ write and send an e-mail
■ send computer files by e-mail
■ build up an address book full of e-mail addresses.

Attachments

● Click on this icon to **attach** any computer file to an e-mail

You will see a window like this.

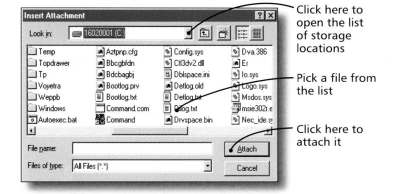

Click here to open the list of storage locations

Pick a file from the list

Click here to attach it

Use this window to find and select the file you wish to attach. Then send the e-mail in the normal way. The file will be sent along with it.

Opening an attached file

If you receive an e-mail with an attachment it will look like this.

This is the attached file

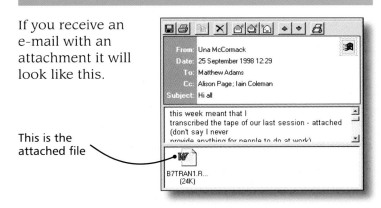

● Double-click on the file icon to open it up and look at it

9 Spreadsheets

This unit is about using spreadsheet software. A spreadsheet can do lots of calculations for you very quickly. It is also very useful for producing graphs and charts.

On Target

In this unit you will learn how to:

- enter numbers and words into a spreadsheet
- make the computer work out the answers to sums
- improve your work with layout and colour
- make graphs and charts from the numbers in a spreadsheet.

Making it all Add Up

Working with numbers is an essential part of everyday life. We're often adding numbers up, taking them away, multiplying and dividing them.

We can do simple sums in our heads. When things get a bit more difficult we reach for paper and a pencil. Then, to speed things up a bit, there is the calculator.

In many situations there's another tool you may be able to use. A **spreadsheet** is even better than a calculator.

What is a Spreadsheet?

Spreadsheets help with series of calculations that need to be repeated often. Once set up they can be used to explore the effect of changing one number on the others. The data from a spreadsheet can also be displayed very easily as a graph or chart.

How might a spreadsheet help the pupils on the right?

- A spreadsheet is a **quick** way of completing a calculation. Using a calculator will save time for them to get on with the rest of their work.

- A spreadsheet is **accurate.** If the pupils enter the right details, they will get the right answer.

- A spreadsheet is **neat** and **tidy.** Like a word processor, a spreadsheet is a good way of improving the presentation of their work.

- A spreadsheet can be **checked** and **corrected.** When they use a spreadsheet, their workings are easy to read through and check. If they find a mistake they can make a correction.

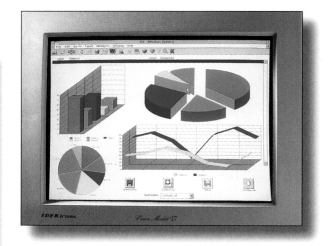

The Contents of a Spreadsheet ■

When you are setting out a spreadsheet you have to enter **Values**, **Labels** and **Formulas**.

Values

When you start a calculation there are numbers that you know already. These are called values. The values are entered into the spreadsheet.

Labels

Labels are words you enter to explain the values. You wouldn't just enter a list of numbers, without any explanation. Putting labels next to each of the numbers makes it easier for your teacher to understand the spreadsheet. It also makes it easier for you to check it through later.

Formulas

Formulas are the sums you enter into spreadsheets. Formulas are how you tell the computer what calculation to do. You will learn how to make formulas on page 132.

To create calculations you use **operators**. These are the signs that you use in a sum. Spreadsheet operators are very similar to the ones in your written sums.

The example used in this book is Microsoft *Excel*. There are other Windows spreadsheet packages available and don't worry if you are using one of these at school – you will find that they work in almost exactly the same way.

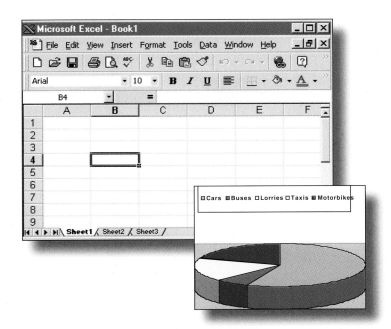

Getting IT Right in...

History

A pupil knows the start and end dates of several wars. He needs to work out how long each war lasted.

Business Studies

A business studies pupil knows the exchange rate between dollars and pounds. He wants to work out how much an item would cost in pounds.

Geography

Some geography pupils take rainfall measurements every day for a week. They want to work out the total rainfall for the week.

WHAT YOU HAVE TO DO

On this page you saw the example of some pupils who wanted to work out the total rainfall during a week.

1. **Where would they get the numbers they need for this calculation?**

2. **What calculation do they have to carry out?**

I. Spreading the work

The first step is to enter the values – the numbers – to be used in your calculation.

Entering values

Whenever you have to do a sum you start with some numbers. These are the **values**. You work out the answer from these values.

The first step in creating a spreadsheet is to enter the values.

You must also enter the titles and labels that explain the purpose of the spreadsheet and the meaning of each of the values.

The tool bar

Opening, saving and printing files

The tool bar contains the same icons for opening, saving and printing a file. You used them when you were word processing.

Resizing and closing

The resize and close buttons are found in the top right hand corner, just like any other window.

Remember the upper buttons are used to close or resize the entire software window. The lower buttons are used to close or resize the work file only.

The spreadsheet window

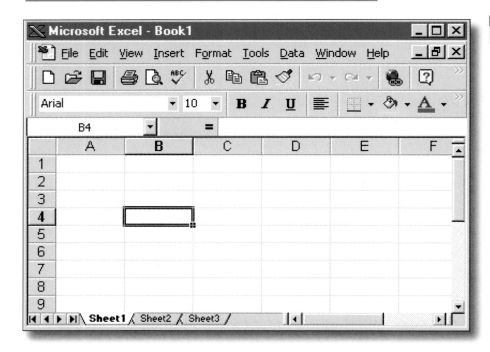

The spreadsheet window has all the typical windows features, including a menu bar, tool bar and working area

The working area

The working area of a spreadsheet package is a grid of rows and columns. The rows are numbered, and the columns have letters. Each box in the grid is named after the column and row in which it is found.

● The boxes are called **cells**.

● The name of a cell is the **cell reference**.

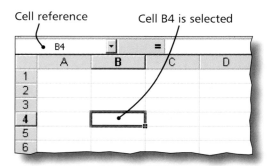

Cell reference

Cell B4 is selected

The spreadsheet pointer ■

When the mouse pointer is placed over the spreadsheet working area it looks like a white cross.

- Select any cell in the spreadsheet by clicking on it with the spreadsheet pointer

Labels and values ■

To make a spreadsheet easy to read you should enter words to tell you what the numbers are. These are called the **labels**.

Then enter the numbers that you want to use in the calculation. These are the **values** mentioned earlier.

Below is a typical spreadsheet, created by a pupil to help with a science experiment.

	A	B	C
1	EFFECTS OF LIGHT ON PLANT GROWTH		
2			
3		Plant 1	Plant 2
4		(White Light)	(Green Light)
5	Height at start (cm)	1.5	1.3
6	Height at end (cm)	3.9	2.4

In this example the **labels** are in blue and the **values** are in red. In your spreadsheet all the text and numbers will be black.

The labels include:

- a title for the whole spreadsheet
- headings for each column of values
- headings for each row of values.

Notice that the pupil has told you what type of measurement was used – centimetres. All the information you need is included in the spreadsheet.

Entering labels and values into cells ■

- Put a label or value into a cell by:
  - selecting the cell with the pointer
  - typing whatever you want to go into the cell

What you have typed is shown at the top of the spreadsheet like this.

The tick button

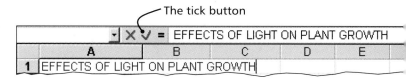

	A	B	C	D	E
1	EFFECTS OF LIGHT ON PLANT GROWTH				

You can make changes to what you have typed.

- Delete and retype as much as you like
- When you are happy with what you have typed, click on the **tick** button

If you make a mistake you can change what you have entered in any cell in the spreadsheet.

- Select a cell. The contents are displayed just as they were when you typed them

  You can:
  - edit the contents
  - type the contents again from scratch
  - press the **Delete** key to clear the cell

Results ◻

On the next page you will see how to use these numbers to work out the results of the experiment.

WHAT YOU HAVE TO DO

1. **Enter all the labels and values needed to set out the calculation in the spreadsheet shown on this page.**

2. **Use a spreadsheet to set up a simple *times-table* chart.**

   ```
   X|1 2 3
   1|1 2 3
   2|2 4 6
   3|3 6 9
   ```

   Save and print your work. Keep a copy in your IT folder.

2. What are your values?

On the last page you worked through the example of a pupil who entered information about the growth of two plants in a science experiment.

Next you will see how formulas can be used to work out the results of the experiment.

Calculations

You have seen how you can create a spreadsheet by adding values and labels. On this page you will learn how to enter **formulas**.

Formulas tell the computer to work out the answer to a calculation. In other words – you enter the sum you want the computer to do, and it shows you the answer.

Label the results

Before you start to enter the formula, make sure that there is a label which will explain what the result means.

	A	B	C
1	EFFECTS OF LIGHT ON PLANT GROWTH		
2			
3		Plant 1	Plant 2
4		(White Light)	(Green Light)
5	Height at start (cm)	1.5	1.3
6	Height at end (cm)	3.9	2.4
7			
8	GROWTH		

This label tells you what the formula will show

The formula will go in here

Think about it first

Think about it before you start. What is the calculation that you want to do?

In this case the pupil wants to work out how high each plant has grown during the experiment. This means:

*The height at the end of the experiment **minus** the height at the start of the experiment.*

Starting a formula

To start a formula:

- Select the cell where you want the formula to be
- Type an equals sign

All formulas start with an equals sign.

In this example you will look at the formula for the first plant, and this goes in **cell B8**.

More complex calculations *p134*

Select the first value

To enter a value into a formula you simply click on the cell containing the value.

Remember the calculation in the example is:

The height at the end of the experiment **minus** the height at the start of the experiment.

So the first value you need is:

The height at the end of the experiment.

This is stored in **cell B6**.

● Click on B6 and the spreadsheet looks like this

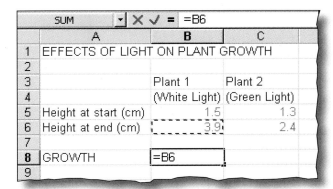

Select the second value

Remember the calculation was:

The height at the end of the experiment **minus** *the height at the start of the experiment.*

So the second value is:

The height at the start of the experiment.

This is stored in **cell B5**.

● Click on cell B5 and the formula looks like this

SUM	▼	✕ ✓ =	=B6-B5	
	A	B	C	
1	EFFECTS OF LIGHT ON PLANT GROWTH			
2				
3		Plant 1	Plant 2	
4		(White Light)	(Green Light)	
5	Height at start (cm)	1.5	1.3	
6	Height at end (cm)	3.9	2.4	
7				
8	GROWTH	=B6-B5		
9				

● Click on the **tick** button to enter the completed formula

Operator, please

Next you will need to enter an **operator**. Operators are signs like **plus** and **minus** which you use in formulas.

Here are the four main operators:

Action	Operator	Symbol
Add	Plus sign	+
Subtract	Minus sign (dash)	-
Multiply	Asterisk	*
Divide	Forward Slash	/

The operator the pupil needs to use in this case is the **minus** sign, or dash.

The result

After you click the tick button you will see the result of the formula. Here is what the spreadsheet would look like with both formulas entered:

	A	B	C	
1	EFFECTS OF LIGHT ON PLANT GROWTH			
2				
3		Plant 1	Plant 2	
4		(White Light)	(Green Light)	
5	Height at start (cm)	1.5	1.3	
6	Height at end (cm)	3.9	2.4	
7				
8	GROWTH	2.4	1.1	

It seems that white light produces greater plant growth than green light.

3. Getting your sums right

On this page there are some more examples of spreadsheet calculations. They demonstrate some of the ways that spreadsheets can be used.

More calculations

There are lots of different sorts of calculations you can do with a spreadsheet. For example:

- calculating money
- dealing with columns of figures
- working out percentages.

As you work through the page, copy these examples using your spreadsheet software. You should also look for examples of similar calculations in your school work, and use spreadsheets to make this work easier.

Currency

In modern spreadsheet packages you can enter **currency** values. Currency means money. To enter a money value, type a pound sign at the start of a number. For example:

£5.00

£4000

Older spreadsheet packages may not complete the calculation if you enter a pound sign when you type in a value. If you have a package like this, enter the values without a pound sign.

Your teacher will tell you which type of spreadsheet package you are using.

More than two cell references

The examples of formulas you looked at on the last page had two cell references each. But you can put as many cell references as you wish into a formula.

Here is an example. A pupil wanted to work out how much money he had. He set up a spreadsheet that showed:

- how much money he had to start with
- how much money he earned
- how much money he spent.

The spreadsheet looked like this:

	A	B
1	MY MONEY	
2		
3	I started with	£ 118.70
4	I earned	£ 62.20
5	I spent	£ 90.00
6		

This spreadsheet accepts currency values

He added a formula to work out how much money he had. The formula worked like this:

*Money he started with **plus** money he earned **minus** money he spent.*

Here is the spreadsheet after he entered the formula:

	A	B
1	MY MONEY	
2		
3	I started with	£ 118.70
4	I earned	£ 62.20
5	I spent	£ 90.00
6	I finished up with	£ 90.90
7		

The answer is shown as currency

Turning results into graphs *p140*

Sums

The formula B3 + B4 – B5 performs this calculation.

In mathematical language **sum** doesn't mean any calculation. It means adding together a set of numbers.

The mathematical symbol for sum is Σ.

There is a tool bar button with this symbol on it. You can use it to quickly add up a column or row of numbers.

Some pupils were monitoring traffic on the busy road in front of their school. Here are the numbers they counted during their lunch hour.

	A	B	C
1	TRAFFIC MONITORING SURVEY		
2	Traffic Passing Main Rd School, 12.00 - 1.30		
3			
4	Private Cars	104	
5	Buses and Coaches	10	
6	Lorries and Vans	27	
7	Taxis	1	
8	Motorbikes	35	
9	TOTAL		

To add up the total (SUM) of all types of traffic:

- Select the cell where the answer goes (B9)
- Click on the SUM button

B9   =   =SUM(B4:B8)

	A	B	C
1	TRAFFIC MONITORING SURVEY		
2	Traffic Passing Main Rd School, 12.00 - 1.30		
3			
4	Private Cars	104	
5	Buses and Coaches	10	
6	Lorries and Vans	27	
7	Taxis	1	
8	Motorbikes	35	
9	TOTAL	177	

Percentages

You can work out a percentage using a spreadsheet.

For example, you often see 'special offers' in the shops. If you buy a pack you get a certain percent extra free. To work out exactly how much extra you get, **multiply** the normal pack size (cell B3) by the percentage extra (cell B4). Here is the result:

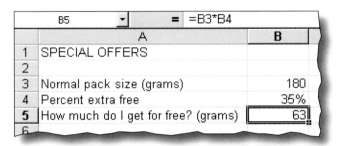

B5   =   =B3*B4

	A	B
1	SPECIAL OFFERS	
2		
3	Normal pack size (grams)	180
4	Percent extra free	35%
5	How much do I get for free? (grams)	63
6		

In modern spreadsheet packages, percentage values can be entered.

- Enter a number followed by the percentage sign. For example:

  50%

  17.5%

Older packages may not be able to complete the calculation if you use a percentage sign. In this case you will need to use a decimal instead. For example:

50%	= 0.5	
5%	= 0.05	
17.5%	= 0.175	

WHAT YOU HAVE TO DO

1. **Copy the examples given on this page into a spreadsheet package.**

2. **Create a spreadsheet to keep account of how you spend your pocket money each week. Calculate how much you spend and how much is left over. How can you extend the spreadsheet for further weeks?**

Save and print out your spreadsheets. Keep your work in your IT folder.

4. Making it look good

On this page you will learn some ways of formatting the contents of a spreadsheet.

Formatting the spreadsheet

The contents of a spreadsheet can be formatted just like the text in a word processed document.

Spreadsheets can be made to look much clearer and more attractive by using suitable colours and text styles.

For example, here is a spreadsheet used to work out the bill in a café.

	A	B
1	La Vie Parisienne	
2	Bistro Café	
3		
4	Table 2	
5		
6	Capuccino	1.75
7	Citron Pressee	1.25
8	Espresso	1.5
9	Croissant	2
10		
11	TOTAL	6.5
12	Service charge not included	

After it has been formatted it can be given to the customer. It presents a good impression of the café.

Selecting a block of cells

To format cells you have to select them. To select cells, simply *drag* the mouse pointer across the cells. They will be highlighted.

Click here to select the entire spreadsheet

To select a whole row click on the row number

To select a whole column click on the column letter

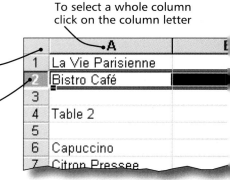

Text colour, size and style

The spreadsheet tool bar gives you formatting tools, just like the ones you used to format a word processed document.

Text and background colour

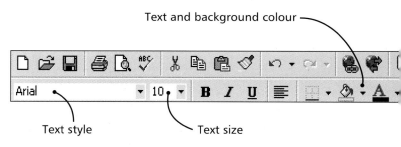

Text style

Text size

If you can't remember how to use these tools, look back to page 56.

Document style p56

Fit to a cell

If a **label** is too big to fit into a cell, it just spills over into the next cell. Look at the headings of the spreadsheets to see this.

But this doesn't work with **numbers** that are too big. And it doesn't work if the next cell has something in it.

This label has been cut off

This means a value is too big to show

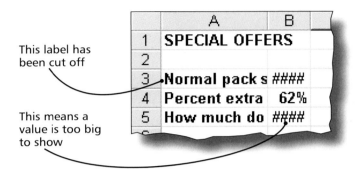

If either of these problems happen, increase the width of the column. To **increase the column width**:

- move the pointer to the line between two columns. It will turn to this symbol:
- drag this symbol so that the line between the columns is dragged along. This increases the column width.

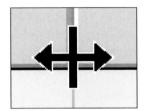

Currency and percentage

If you have entered values as ordinary numbers, you can change them to currency (pounds) or percentages.

Simply select the cells and then click on these buttons on the tool bar.

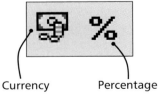

Currency   Percentage

Remember that percentages are equivalent to decimal numbers. So 50% is the same as 0.5.

IT at work

People in all kinds of businesses make use of spreadsheets to help them with their work.

They often need to work out:

- how much it will cost them to complete a task, or get goods ready for sale
- how much they can charge a customer for that task, or for those goods
- how much profit they might make
- how much money they need to spend to pay bills and buy raw materials.

These types of calculation have to be carried out all the time in a typical business. Spreadsheets are used to make it easier and quicker to get accurate answers to these important questions.

La Vie Parisienne Bistro Café

Croissant	50p
Potage légumes	£2.50
Salade de tomates	£3.50
Sancisson à l'Ail	£3.50
Frites	£1.00
Omelette	£3.00
Vin de ttable	£1.50
Café express	£1.50

WHAT YOU HAVE TO DO

1. **Enter the café menu spreadsheet shown on this page. Format it in any way you choose to produce an attractive bill for customers.**

2. **Change the format of one of the spreadsheets you have created while doing this unit. Try several alternative formats, and compare their suitability.**

Save and/or print out your work and keep it in your IT folder.

137

5. Over and over again

**Spreadsheets can be used to ask questions, such as
What if...?, *How much...?* and *What happened...?***

**On this page you will see how the spreadsheets you have
created can be used to work out the answer to questions.**

Answering questions

There are many ways in which a spreadsheet is
better than an ordinary calculator. You have
seen a few of the advantages which a
spreadsheet offers:

- setting out your work
- letting you save and print your calculations
- reformatting the spreadsheet like a word
  processed document.

On this page you will look at one other
important difference – once you have set up a
spreadsheet you can use it over and over again.
You can change the values and the computer
will work out the new answers for you. Think
how handy that is. Once you have set up a
useful spreadsheet you can use it as many
times as you like with new numbers.

And it means that you can use spreadsheets to
answer questions. What would happen if a
value changed? How high can a value get?

Know all about IT

The spreadsheet was first developed in 1979. It was
called *VisiCalc*, and was very successful. It was
written by a student at Harvard Business School.

VisiCalc helped create
the need for personal
computers. At the time
roughly a quarter of all
Apple computers were
bought by businesses
solely to
run *VisiCalc*.

Entering new values

To enter new values into a spreadsheet you select the
cell and retype the value.

Be careful not to type over one of the formulas.

What if...?

What if the special offer changed?

This spreadsheet was set up to work out how much
extra you would get from a special offer:

By changing the percentage extra you can use this
spreadsheet to check *What if the special offer changed?*

SPECIAL OFFERS	
Normal pack size (grams)	180
Percent extra free	20%
How much do I get for free? (gram	36

SPECIAL OFFERS	
Normal pack size (grams)	180
Percent extra free	62%
How much do I get for free? (grams)	111.6

How much can I spend?

On page 134 you saw how a pupil used a spreadsheet to work out how much money he had. He used three values to work out the answer.

| B6 | ▼ | = | =B3+B4-B5 |

	A	B	C
1	MY MONEY		
2			
3	I started with	£ 118.70	
4	I earned	£ 62.20	
5	I spent	£ 49.50	
6	I finished up with	£ 131.40	

By changing any of these values he can make tests and see what would happen. For example he could test what would happen if he missed his Saturday job and didn't earn anything at all.

	A	B
1	MY MONEY	
2		
3	I started with	£ 118.70
4	I earned	£ 62.20
5	I spent	£ 90.00
6	I finished up with	£ 90.90
7		

£90.00 is too much to spend!

Or he could ask this question *How much can I spend, and still have £100 left?*

He could keep trying out different numbers.

	A	B
1	MY MONEY	
2		
3	I started with	£ 118.70
4	I earned	£ 62.20
5	I spent	£ 80.90
6	I finished up with	£ 100.00
7		

£80.90 is the most he can spend

Whenever you have a spreadsheet you can try out different values and see what effect this has on the result.

What happened the next day?

A spreadsheet was set up to record the traffic passing a school.

	A	B
1	TRAFFIC MONITORING SURVEY	
2	Traffic Passing Main Rd School, 12.0	
3		
4	Private Cars	87
5	Buses and Coaches	12
6	Lorries and Vans	35
7	Taxis	2
8	Motorbikes	28
9		
10	TOTAL	164
11		

TRAFFIC MONITORING SURVEY
Traffic Passing Main Rd School, 12.00 - 1.30

Private Cars	104
Buses and Coaches	10
Lorries and Vans	27
Taxis	1
Motorbikes	35
TOTAL	177

The same spreadsheet could be used the next day to record the same information.

WHAT YOU HAVE TO DO

Open one of the spreadsheets you have made while working through this unit.

Think of one or more questions you can answer using this spreadsheet.

Vary values in the spreadsheet to answer the question(s).

Print out the resulting spreadsheets, so that you have a permanent record of the answers. Keep your work in your IT folder.

6. Say it with graphs

On this page you will see how graphs can be used to show results from spreadsheets. Graphs and charts will help other people to make sense of your figures.

Graphs get the message across

You know how to use a spreadsheet to record values and give you answers to questions. You also need to be able to communicate the results – to tell people what your spreadsheet shows.

A famous saying is that *a picture is worth a thousand words*. A **graph** is a picture showing a set of values. It is often easier to understand a graph than to read a table of numbers.

On the next page you will learn how to make spreadsheet graphs yourself.

What values?

Your spreadsheet might have lots of values in it. You don't have to use them all to make a graph. Carefully choose the figures you use to make the graph.

Ask yourself *What is my graph about?* Make sure you know what you want to show in the graph.

When you have decided which values to use **select** the cells.

What values?

For example, at Main Road School the pupils counted traffic and stored the results in a spreadsheet. You saw it on page 135. They kept on counting traffic every day for a week, and made a larger spreadsheet which showed all these results.

	A	B	C	D	E	F	G
1	TRAFFIC SURVEY						
2	Traffic passing Main Rd School, 12.00 - 1.30						
3							
4		Mon	Tue	Wed	Thur	Fri	TOTAL
5	Private Cars	104	87	120	99	79	489
6	Buses and Coaches	10	12	11	10	11	54
7	Lorries and Vans	27	35	41	32	20	155
8	Taxis	1	2	0	2	0	5
9	Motorbikes	35	28	33	36	31	163
10	TOTAL	177	164	205	179	141	

One pupil wanted to make a graph showing how the total amount of traffic changed from day to day. He selected these cells.

	A	B	C	D	E	F	G
1	TRAFFIC SURVEY						
2	Traffic passing Main Rd School, 12.00 - 1.30						
3							
4		Mon	Tue	Wed	Thur	Fri	TOTAL
5	Private Cars	104	87	120	99	79	489
6	Buses and Coaches	10	12	11	10	11	54
7	Lorries and Vans	27	35	41	32	20	155
8	Taxis	1	2	0	2	0	5
9	Motorbikes	35	28	33	36	31	163
10	TOTAL	177	164	205	179	141	

One pupil wanted to show how the traffic was divided between different types of vehicle. She selected these cells.

	A	B	C	D	E	F	G
1	TRAFFIC SURVEY						
2	Traffic passing Main Rd School, 12.00 - 1.30						
3							
4		Mon	Tue	Wed	Thur	Fri	TOTAL
5	Private Cars	104	87	120	99	79	489
6	Buses and Coaches	10	12	11	10	11	54
7	Lorries and Vans	27	35	41	32	20	155
8	Taxis	1	2	0	2	0	5
9	Motorbikes	35	28	33	36	31	163
10	TOTAL	177	164	205	179	141	
11							

What type of graph?

It is important to pick the right type of graph.

If you want to show how a value changes over time, then use a **line graph**.

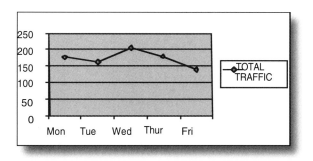

If you want to show how a total is divided up into parts, use a **pie chart**.

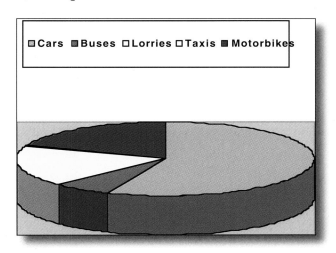

If you want to compare different values with each other, then use a **histogram** (sometimes called a **bar chart**).

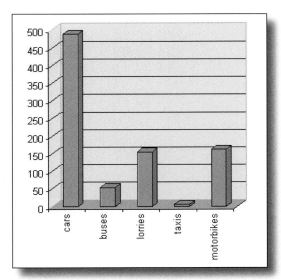

Copy and paste

In Unit 2 you learned how to copy and paste items into your documents. Remember you can use the same techniques to copy and paste part of a spreadsheet, or a spreadsheet graph. Placing a graph directly into some text can improve the document and make the graph easier to understand.

IT at work

Company reports often include facts and figures shown as graphics. This makes them easier to understand

WHAT YOU HAVE TO DO

Pick an interesting spreadsheet which you have created on your course.

You are going to make a graph from this spreadsheet. But first you must decide:

■ what is the graph going to show?

■ what values are you going to use to make the graph?

■ what type of graph are you going to pick?

■ what will the title of your graph be?

Make notes to answer all of these questions. You may like to write on a print-out of the spreadsheet, marking the numbers you want to use.

Keep your work in your IT folder.

7. It's magic!

On the final page in this unit you will learn how to create different spreadsheet graphs and charts.

You will need to decide which type is the most effective for the information you want to communicate.

Create a spreadsheet graph

Modern spreadsheet packages make it very easy to create graphs.

It is so quick that it doesn't matter if it takes you a few tries to get it right. Keep trying until you get just the graph you want.

The tips on this page should make it easy for you to have a go.

Select the cells

Remember – to select cells you *drag* the mouse pointer over the cells.

Don't just select the numbers. Select the labels which go with the numbers. Sometimes this is easy because the labels are next to the numbers.

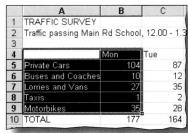

	A	B	C
1	TRAFFIC SURVEY		
2	Traffic passing Main Rd School, 12.00 - 1.3		
3			
4		Mon	Tue
5	Private Cars	104	87
6	Buses and Coaches	10	12
7	Lorries and Vans	27	35
8	Taxis	1	2
9	Motorbikes	35	28
10	TOTAL	177	164

If the labels and values are in different parts of the spreadsheet, you can still select them.

	A	B	C	D	E	F	G
1	TRAFFIC SURVEY						
2	Traffic passing Main Rd School, 12.00 - 1.30						
3							
4		Mon	Tue	Wed	Thur	Fri	TOTAL
5	Private Cars	104	87	120	99	79	489
6	Buses and Coaches	10	12	11	10	11	54
7	Lorries and Vans	27	35	41	32	20	155
8	Taxis	1	2	0	2	0	5
9	Motorbikes	35	28	33	36	31	163
10	TOTAL	177	164	205	179	141	

- Hold down the **Control** key while you drag the pointer over each selection

Graph Wizard

To help you make graphs, modern spreadsheets have a tool called the *Graph Wizard*.

- Click on this icon on the tool bar

Pick a graph

The graph wizard works differently in different spreadsheet packages. Don't worry if yours doesn't work exactly like this.

Here is the first screen of a typical graph wizard.

Pick the type of graph you want

More choices

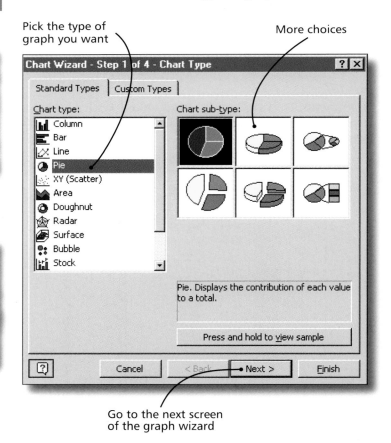

Go to the next screen of the graph wizard

Putting graphs into documents *p70*

Here is another screen of a graph wizard.

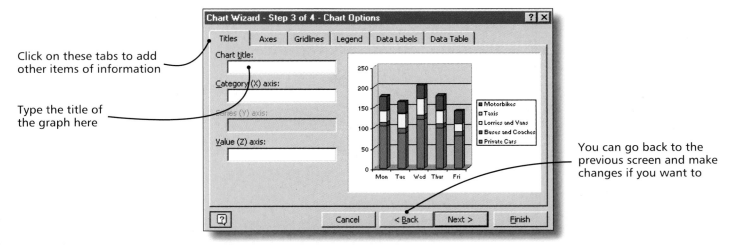

Click on these tabs to add other items of information

Type the title of the graph here

You can go back to the previous screen and make changes if you want to

Here is another example, from a different graph.

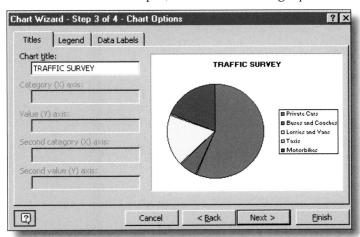

Place the graph

The graph is shown in the spreadsheet. You can drag it to a new position so that it doesn't cover up the numbers.

Resize handles

On Target

After you have worked through this unit you should be able to:

- enter numbers and words into a spreadsheet
- make the computer work out the answers to sums
- improve your work with layout and colour
- make graphs and charts from the numbers in a spreadsheet.

WHAT YOU HAVE TO DO

1. **Create two or more different graphs from a spreadsheet using a graph wizard.**

2. **Compare the results.**

   - **Which is the clearest?**
   - **Which is the most eye-catching?**

Index

A
address book, *see* e-mail

B
backup   17
bookmark   115
bullet points, *see* style

C
calculations, *see* spreadsheets
CD-ROM   92–97, *see also*
   storage
cell, *see* spreadsheets
cell reference, *see* spreadsheets
charts, *see* spreadsheets
clip art   66, 67
close (exit)
   file   27, 55
   software   25, 27, 40, 55
CPU (Central Processing Unit),
   see processor
colour
   in graphics   42, 43
   in logo   88, 89
   in text   56, 136
control   6, 80–91
copy
   file   29
   graphics   48, 49, 70, 141
   software   29
copyright   67
cursor   52
cut   48, 49, 70

D
databases   100, 101
   field   100, 101
   record   100, 101
   table   100, 101
delete
   file   29
   graphics   47
   text   58
desktop   22, 41
   icons   22
   recycle bin   29
   Start button   22, 25
   task bar   22, 25
drag, *see* move

E
e-mail   7, 116–127
   address book   125
   attach   119, 127
   folders   120
   read   124
   receive   123
   reply   126
   send   122, 126, 127
   write   117

equal opportunities   18, 19
exit, *see* close

F
field, *see* databases
file   16, 23, 24
file name   16, 36, 54
file server   11, 30
floppy disk, *see* storage
folder   23, 120
fonts, *see* style
formulas, *see* spreadsheets

G
graphics   6, 12, 32–49, *see*
   also colour, style
   adding text to graphics   44
   adding graphics to slides,
      see presentation
   bitmap packages   46
   creating graphics   34, 35
   in Logo   89–91
   vector packages   47
graphs, *see* spreadsheets

H
hard disk, *see* storage
hardware   4, 5, 8, 47
health and safety   14, 15

I
icons   21, 24, *see also* desktop
information search   7, 92–101
insert
   graphics   66
   text   52, 58
interface   20–31
   alternative interfaces   20,
      31
   CD-ROM interface   94
   graphical user interface   20
   user interface   6, 20, 21
   W.I.M.P.   20
   Windows interface   13, 20,
      30, 31
Internet   7, 9, 102–115

K
keyboard   4, 9, 52, 53
keys   53
key words   110

L
links   106
load, *see* open
Logo (turtle)   81–91

M
menu   21, 26, 45, 55
menu bar   26

monitor/VDU   4, 9
mouse   4, 9, 21, 35
move (drag)
   file   28, 29
   graphics   48, 67, 71
multimedia   72, 73, 92–99

N
navigation bar   95
network   9, 11
new   40, 54

O
open (load, start up)
   CD-ROM   94
   file   41, 54, 70
   software   13, 24, 34, 68, 74
   web site   114

P
password   11, 17
paste   48, 49, 70, 71, 141
pointer   21, 52, 131
presentation   6, 64–79
   adding audio   72, 76
   adding graphics   75
   adding sound   72, 76
   adding video   72, 76
   giving a presentation   78,
      79
   slides   75
   templates   74, 75
print   37, 55, 87, 114, 125
printer   5, 9
processor   4, 9

R
record, *see* databases
recycle bin, *see* desktop
resize
   graphics   67, 71
   text box   44
   window   27
restore   29

S
save   9, 17, 36, 37, 54, 114,
   124
save as   37, 55
scroll bar   27
search   96, *see also*
   information search
search engine   108, 109
security   16, 17
select
   file   48
   graphics, part of   46, 47,
      48, 70
   text   58, 136
   web site   115

select all   70
software, types of   12, 13
spell check   60
spreadsheets   7, 12, 128–143
   calculations   132–135
   cell   130
   cell reference   130
   charts   141–143
   formulas   129, 132
   graphs   140–143
   labels   129, 131, 132
   values   129, 131, 133
Start button, *see* desktop
start up, *see* open
storage   10, 12, 23
   CD-ROM   4, 10
   floppy disk   4, 10, 29
   hard disk   10
   Zip drive   11
style
   adding styles to graphics
      38, 39
   bullet points   57
   fonts   45, 56
   number lists   57
   text formats   56, 58, 136,
      137
   text layout   62, 63
   text sizes   57, 136

T
table, *see* databases
task bar, *see* desktop
text formats, *see* style
title bar   26
toggles   56
tool bar   27, 35, 56, 107, 130
turtle, *see* Logo

U
undo   39, 59
URL (Uniform Resource
   Locator)   105, 115
user interface, *see* interface

V
VDU (Visual Display Unit), *see*
   monitor
virus   15

W
web browser   12, 104
web site   102, 114
window   20, 26, 52, 82, 120
Windows interface, *see*
   interface
word processing   6, 12, 50–63
World Wide Web   102